LIBRARY OF AMERICAN
INDIAN HISTORY

Night of the Cruel Moon

Cherokee Removal and the Trail of Tears

Stan Hoig

Facts On File, Inc.

AN INFOBASE HOLDINGS COMPANY

To Pat, to whom I owe so much.

Facts On File, Inc.
11 Penn Plaza
New York, NY 10001

Library of Congress Cataloging-in-Publication Data
Hoig, Stan
   Night of the cruel moon : Cherokee removal and the Trail of Tears
/ by Stan Hoig.
    p. cm.
   Includes bibliographical references (p.) and index.
   Summary: A narrative history of the removal by white Americans of
the Cherokee peoples from their eastern homeland to the Indian
territory now known as Oklahoma.
   ISBN 0-8160-3307-2 (HB)
   ISBN 0-8160-3491-5 (PB)
   1. Trail of Tears, 1838—Juvenile literature. 2. Cherokee. 3. Cherokee
Indians—Relocation—Juvenile literature. [1. Trail of Tears,
1838. 2. Cherokee Indians—History. 3. Indians of North America—
Southern States—History.]   I. Title. Indians—History—19th century—
Juvenile literature.
E99.C5H73 1996
976.6'004975—dc20   95-22039

Text design by Robert Yaffe
Cover design by Amy Beth Gonzalez

This book is printed on acid-free paper.

Printed in the United States of America

MP FOF 10 9 8 7 6 5 4 3 2 1

Contents

It was a night of dark design.
They said farewell to all they loved;
And driven off to lands afar,
They left behind a trail of tears
Beneath a cold, cruel moon

                                    —swh

Foreword

The term "Trail of Tears" originally referred to the forced removal of the Cherokees from their native habitat in the South to the Indian Territory, now Oklahoma. Today, however, it has come to represent the exiling of many Native American tribes east of the Mississippi to the West. The term is symbolic of the entire period of white takeover of Indian lands conducted during the eighteenth and nineteenth centuries, first by the British and later by the various states and by the United States government.

In its real meaning, therefore, the term conveys far more than the pathetic march of Indian people west. The removal of the tribes from their established habitat reaches back to their first contact with European settlers. The Cherokee ordeal typifies the chicanery and duplicity that officials employed to drive the Indian tribes from their treaty-recognized lands, as well as the often brutal advantage taken of Native Americans by some white Americans.

The events of the removal cast the shadow of villainy on the Jackson and Van Buren administrations and on many of the white people of the day. Still, recorded history should not overlook the fact that there were also white citizens and government officials who wanted to do right by the Indians. Sad to say, there weren't enough of them.

Perhaps the most important lesson to be drawn from the saga of Indian removal is that it is not an event of the past isolated from the present. Over a century and a half have passed since removal, but much of the Jacksonian-day prejudice against Native Americans still exists socially and economically. The situation is improving, but many tribal people in America are still living under repressed conditions and are still subjected to much societal bias. Today's formally educated Indians are far more adept at fighting to restore some of the rights and property once taken from them by spurious means. Still, it is no exaggeration to say that in sociological and economic terms the Indian even yet walks a Trail of Tears.

While this book draws on much information that has long been known about the Trail of Tears, it makes some significant deviations. This is particularly so in relation to the routes to the west taken by the various removal groups. A careful review of removal records revealed that some important clues regarding the routes had been overlooked in previous accounts. Though this study uncovered many of these deviations on its own, it was aided considerably by the National Park Service's thorough and detailed study of the removal routes.

I wish to extend my appreciation to Oleta Kite, Margie Johnson Lowe, and Marguerite Turner for their help; to Mary C. Young of the Trail of Tears National Historic Trails Committee; to Archivist Bill Welge and the staff of the Archives/Manuscripts Division, Oklahoma Historical Society; to the National Archives; to the staff of the University of Central Oklahoma Library; to Dan Smith and Donna Kerr of the University of Central Oklahoma Photo Services; and to my wife, Patricia Corbell Hoig, for her ever-generous editorial assistance.

In the Path of Empire

Teams and wagons by the hundreds began pulling into position along the Hiwassee River near Charleston, Tennessee on the morning of October 1, 1838. The forested hills were still dressed in their summer green, but the trees sagged limply in the cold, drizzling rain. The gray, overcast sky added to the deep sense of gloom that lay over the entire caravan as the Cherokees quietly said their goodbyes.

They shook hands with those who would soon follow and tearfully embraced those who were too ill or infirm to travel. Despair etched the numb faces of old and young alike. They had done all that could be done to avoid this day. But now it had come. The United States was forcing them to leave their homes and move to a far-off land beyond the Mississippi River.

The first caravan of wagons and carriages pulled into position, and the final loading began. This was the vanguard of several groups that would follow closely in line at intervals during the coming weeks. Some 12,000 people would be transported west. William Shorey Coodey, a schooled tribesman who until only recently had been serving the Cherokee Nation in Washington, D.C., witnessed the departure with great emotion. Coodey, writing to his sisters, could not restrain the intense bitterness in his heart.

Though only one-eighth Cherokee, Chief John Ross proved to be a determined political fighter against removal to the West. *(Archives & Manuscripts, Oklahoma Historical Society)*

Pangs of parting are tearing the hearts of our bravest
men at this forced abandonment of their dear lov'd country. . . . Wretched indeed must be that individual who
can fold his arms and look with composure upon scenes
like these. I envy not such a being, but despise, aye,
loathe him from my very soul whether *white* or *red*.

Finally the wagons were ready to roll. Principal Chief John
Ross, small in stature but large in presence, climbed on a wagon
box. Instinctively, the people gathered around this man who had
fought so hard for them and who was clearly the most beloved
leader of their nation. Ross said a brief prayer of hope for God's
guidance. The people said their amens and turned away.

A bugle sounded, and the great exodus began. It would be a
fateful journey for all and a deadly one for many. Hardly had the
drivers lashed their teams into action and the wagons lurched
forward when the entourage heard a low rumble of thunder ahead
of them to the west. Everyone looked in that direction. A black
cloud was spiraling above the horizon. Suddenly the cloud disappeared, and the sky became clear again.

A soft murmur of pain rose from the wagons. It was an omen,
many said, an omen portending some great misfortune awaiting
them ahead. Coodey himself was shaken. In the thunder he felt he
could hear "a voice of divine indignation for the wrongs of my
poor and unhappy countrymen, driven by brutal power from all
they loved and cherished in the land of their fathers to gratify the
cravings of avarice."

The wagons rattled on, moving slowly up the Hiwassee on the
first leg of a historic migration to a distant region known as Indian
Territory, which today is the state of Oklahoma. The journey was
destined to be an epic travail of misery and death that the
Cherokees would call the *nuna dat shun'yi*, the "Trail Where They
Cried." It would become known to history as the Trail of Tears.

The Cherokees, their number estimated at about 22,000, had
existed as hunters, gatherers, and planters before the white man
came. Their nation covered a vast, pristine domain of mountains,
woodlands, and streams. It encompassed portions of what are

today the states of Virginia, Kentucky, Tennessee, North and South Carolina, Georgia, and Alabama. To protect their proprietorship of this immense, game-rich hunting ground and homeland, they had fought wars with the Shawnees and other tribes to the north and the Muscogees to the south. They called themselves the *Ani'-Yun'wiya*, the Principal People. They were the Cherokees.

How long they had been there, they themselves did not know. Tribal traditions told them that their ancestors had come out of the ground. The Cherokees lived in small villages along rivers, traveled by canoe and on foot, and raised their families in pole-and-thatch huts. They regularly sent forth warring and hunting parties, celebrated battle victories, and conducted annual tribal rites. They held dances, engaged in lacrosse-style ball play, and competed at foot races, eagerly wagering on the results.

The Cherokees governed themselves with a combination of civil heads and war leaders. Each town had its own council and chiefs who met regularly in domed, earth-covered meeting lodges to discuss matters of concern. The people subsisted on the produce of the earth: game that they killed, berries and roots gathered from the forest, and maize, potatoes, and melons planted in fields near their homes. They knew no other life and wanted no other.

The Cherokees, it is believed, met their first Europeans in 1540. In that year the army of the Spanish explorer Hernando de Soto passed through their country in search of gold. Fortunately for the Cherokees, they had none; and the often brutal Spaniards soon marched away to the west. During the following century, Cherokee contact with the British began. In 1634, men of the Virginia Colony attacked a Cherokee village near present-day Richmond. The Cherokees defeated the Virginians, forcing them to seek a treaty of friendship.

Traders James Needham and Gabriel Arthur initiated an era of peaceful trade relations when they arrived among the Cherokee Overhill settlements along the Little Tennessee River in 1673. The Overhill Cherokees—so called because they lived west of the Allegheny Mountains—were the dominant body of three principal town groups. These also included the Middle Cherokees of far

Trail of Tears marker, New Echota, Georgia.   *(Photo by Stan Hoig)*

eastern Tennessee and western North Carolina, and the Lower Cherokees of South Carolina and Georgia.

Needham and Arthur were among the first to introduce European goods to the tribespeople. From this visit sprang a period of trade and contact between the Cherokees and the colonies of Virginia and South Carolina that would greatly alter their tribal way of life.

The visit in 1730 of a brazen and energetic young Englishman named Sir Alexander Cuming brought more change for the Cherokees. Cuming's demand that the Cherokees provide one principal chief for him to talk to influenced them in changing from a governmental system of independent town chiefs to that of a single dominant tribal chief. This greatly aided the British in working out trade agreements and treaties. The royalty-minded Englishmen dubbed the head chief "king" or "emperor," but the Cherokees often called him their "Beloved Man."

Cuming also persuaded six Cherokee leaders to accompany him across the Atlantic to visit the English king. One of these was the young Attakullakulla, or the Little Carpenter, who later would rise to importance both as a war leader and a political diplomat. Under his leadership, the Cherokees developed strong trading ties with the colonies. Their dealings, however, were not always happy.

"The traders are very cross with us Indians," Attakullakulla complained to North Carolina governor James Glen. "Do what we can, the white people will cheat us in our weights and measures."

When the British came to him to request the help of Cherokee warriors during the French and Indian War, Attakullakulla reminded them of their promise to build a fort in the Overhill country to protect them from raids by other tribes. "I have a hatchet ready," he said, "but we hope our friends will not expect us to take it up until we have a place of safety for our wives and children."

In 1756 British troops from South Carolina arrived to begin building Fort Loudoun at the juncture of the Tellico and Little

Old Fort Loudoun restoration, Vonore, Tennessee. *(Photo by Stan Hoig)*

Tennessee rivers. For three years the fort provided the Cherokees the protection requested by Attakullakulla. But in 1759, newly appointed Governor William Lyttelton of South Carolina violated his pledge of safe conduct to a delegation of Cherokee chiefs, holding them as hostages at Fort Prince George, South Carolina. A Cherokee attempt to rescue them resulted in the killing of several of the chiefs by the fort's garrison.

The affair ignited a general Cherokee uprising. With the British presence no longer desired, Fort Loudoun was put under siege. Commanding officer Captain Paul Demere was eventually forced to seek a truce and abandon the fort. The Cherokees promised the British soldiers and their families safe conduct. But as the troops departed, the Cherokees discovered that Demere had buried some of the guns and ammunition that he had promised to turn over to them. Infuriated, they attacked and killed or captured many in the retreating garrison.

The British responded with severe assaults on the virtually undefended Cherokee towns in South Carolina, Tennessee, and Georgia. The English commander reported:

> All their towns, amounting to fifteen in number, besides
> many little villages and scattered homes, have been
> burnt; upwards of 1400 acres of corn, according to mod-
> erate computation, entirely destroyed; and near 5000
> Cherokees, including men, women and children, driven
> to the mountains to starve; their only subsistence for
> some time past, being horseflesh.

The Cherokees were forced to repledge their loyalty to the Crown. Throughout the British colonial period, a series of treaties were enacted with the Cherokees. Each one further restricted the Cherokee domain. But it was following the American Revolutionary War that white intrusion and demands for Cherokee land accelerated greatly.

Attakullakulla and the famous chief Oconostota had both become very old. Early in the 1770s, they were succeeded in office by Corn Tassel (or Old Tassel). A benevolent man, Tassel often spoke with great wisdom as he tried to maintain peaceful relations

NANCY WARD, THE CHEROKEE WAR WOMAN

Nancy Ward, the Cherokee War Woman, is one of the most memorable people in Cherokee lore. Her fame rests not only on her role as a heroic battle figure but also on her willingness to oppose the hostile inclinations of her own people. Today, a stone marker stands in tribute over her hilltop grave alongside Highway 411 just south of Benton, Tennessee.

Nancy was born in 1738. A niece of the great chief Attakullakulla, she gained tribal notoriety during the Cherokee-Creek battle of Taliwa in 1755. As a seventeen-year-old girl, she accompanied her husband Kingfisher into battle. Lying behind a log, she helped him reload his rifle. When he was killed, she took up his weapon and aggressively continued the fight in his stead.

By virtue of her fighting valor, Nancy was accorded a place in the council house at Chota, the Cherokee capital city. She remarried, this time to an Irish trader named Brian Ward. A domestic leader, she was the first among the Cherokees to raise cattle. Her people showed their great respect by bestowing on her the title of Ghigua, or Beloved Woman.

Despite her reputation as a warrior, Nancy Ward strongly believed in finding peaceful solutions to conflicts arising from white intrusion. One of her most notable acts came during the American Revolutionary War. In 1776, a Cherokee war faction that favored the British conducted a raid against white settlements in eastern Tennessee. Two prisoners, a white woman and a young man, were brought to Tuskegee. Following the old Cherokee war custom, they were tied to stakes for burning.

Even as the fires were lighted, Nancy Ward defied the angry warriors. She went to the mound of the white woman and cut her ropes. She was unable to save the young man, Samuel Moore, who became the last captive the Cherokees would burn at the stake. Before returning home, the white woman, Mrs. William Bean, taught the Cherokees how to make butter.

During the winter of 1780–81, a North Carolina militia army invaded Cherokee country to put down the war faction that had been striking at frontier settlements. Militia commander

Nancy Ward grave marker near Benton, Tennessee. *(Photo by Stan Hoig)*

Colonel Arthur Campbell noted in his report that "the famous Indian woman Nancy Ward" had arrived at his camp bringing an overture for peace from some of the Cherokee chiefs.

Her position was such that at the Treaty of Hopewell in 1785, she spoke on a chieftain's level to U.S. commissioners.

"I am fond of hearing that there is a peace," she said, "and I hope you have now taken us by the hand in real friendship."

Nancy Ward's reputation followed her into old age. To the end, she steadfastly encouraged her fellow Cherokees to remain at peace. As a prosperous cattle raiser, she was a model of enterprise for other Cherokees. Although too infirm at the age of seventy-nine to attend the meeting of a Cherokee treaty council in 1817, she was the lead signer, along with other Cherokee women, of a plea to the Cherokee chiefs not to sell any more Cherokee land but to continue living on it and raise corn and cotton.

Nancy Ward lived until 1822, dying at the age of eighty-four in present-day Polk County, Tennessee. The stone monument, with its bronze tablet and iron-rail fence, was placed above her grave in 1923 by the Daughters of the American Revolution.

with the whites. Peace, however, was hard to come by in the face of continued conflicts between Cherokee warriors and whites. Anglo-American settlements were rapidly advancing onto Cherokee land along the Watauga, French Broad, Nolichucky, and other rivers that fed westward through the Allegheny Mountains.

The advent of the American Revolution marked an important turning point in Cherokee history. The Cherokees had maintained their affiliation with the British during the war. Their war faction struck back at the ever-increasing intrusions onto their land. At the same time, Corn Tassel and other peace advocates were working to achieve a peaceful relationship with the whites. Each time a new treaty was made with individual states or with the new federal government, the chiefs were induced into signing away more and more of the Cherokee domain.

One of those strongly siding with the British was war leader Dragging Canoe, son of Attakullakulla. He had been furious when in March 1775 his father and others sold the Cherokee lands in Kentucky to Richard Henderson and the Transylvania Company at Sycamore Shoals, Tennessee. Then Dragging Canoe had pointed toward the north and warned Henderson: "You have bought a fair land, but you will find its settlement dark and bloody."

He backed up his threat by leading fierce attacks against the advancing line of white homesteads, block houses, and forts. Frontier militia retaliated, driving Dragging Canoe and his followers southward down the Tennessee River. He established a new stronghold along Chickamauga Creek near present-day Chattanooga, where he and his warriors became known as the dreaded Chickamaugan Cherokees. Corn Tassel and his chiefs remained on the Little Tennessee with their followers and continued to hope for peace.

In 1777 Tassel and other chiefs met with commissioners of North Carolina and the United States at the Long Island of the Holston River. There they were promised that "no white man shall be suffered to reside in or pass through the said Overhill towns without a sufficient certificate signed by three justices of the

THE WISDOM OF CORN TASSEL

From the speech of Principal Chief Corn Tassel at the Treaty of Long Island in July 1777:

It is a little surprising that when we enter into treaties with our brothers, the whites, their whole cry is *more land!*

Many proposals have been made to us to adopt your laws, your religion, your manners and your customs. But, we confess that we do not see the propriety, or practicability of such a reformation, and should be better pleased with beholding the good effects of these doctrines in your own practices than with hearing you talk about them, or reading your papers to us upon such subjects.

The great God of Nature has placed us in different situations. It is true that he has endowed you with many superior advantages; but he has not created us to be your slaves. *We are a separate people!* He has given each their land, under distinct considerations and circumstances; he has stocked yours with cows, ours with buffaloe; yours with hog, ours with bear; yours with sheep, ours with deer. He has, indeed, given you an advantage in this, that your cattle are tame and domestic while ours are wild and demand not only a larger space for range, but art to hunt and kill them; they are, nevertheless, as much our property as other animals are yours, and ought not to be taken away without our consent, or for something equivalent.

peace." It was an empty promise at best. This agreement was followed by the Treaty of Hopewell of 1785, in which the government pledged that the Cherokees would be under the protection of the United States; that any white citizen who settled in their country could be punished by the Indians as they saw fit; and that the Cherokees could send a deputy to Congress to represent their needs.

The conflict was intensified by the founding of the unsanctioned State of Franklin by North Carolina men under John "Nolichucky Jack" Sevier. Sevier organized a ragtag, undisciplined militia that raided the Overhill towns, killing, burning, and looting. Cherokee warriors in turn struck back against white settlements. In one such instance, a Cherokee war party massacred a family named Kirk, who had taken up residence just south of present-day Knoxville.

Sevier and his militia were even then on a raid through the Overhill country, having attacked and destroyed the Cherokee town of Citico and others on the Hiwassee River. From the Hiwassee, Sevier turned north to the Little Tennessee. He went into camp near Corn Tassel's home village of Toquo. Sevier was away from his camp when one of his officers, Major James Hubbard, went to the home of Corn Tassel. A United States flag flew in front of the chief's house. It had been given to him at the Treaty of Hopewell as a promise of good faith and protection by the United States.

Hubbard said he wanted Tassel to attend a council at the house of Chief Old Abraham (or Abram) across the river. He promised safety for the chief and offered him a white flag of truce. Tassel did not trust the officer, but the safety of his people was at stake, so he and his son agreed to accompany Hubbard. Carrying the white flag, they rode the ferry across the river to Abraham's house, where other Cherokee chiefs had already gathered.

Tassel and his son had no sooner taken their seats than militiamen sprang forth to guard the doors and windows. Then a young white man appeared. He was a member of the Kirk family, and he held a war ax in his hand. Corn Tassel and the others knew their end had come. One by one they were axed to death. The *Maryland Gazette* of Annapolis reacted with great indignation:

> They [the chiefs] came under the protection of a flag of truce, a protection inviolable even amongst the most barbarous people, and in the character of ambassadors, a character held sacred by the law and custom of nations, and by the consent of mankind in every age; but under this character, with the sacred protection of a flag, they were attacked and murdered.

The assassination of Corn Tassel made it evident that the Cherokees could no longer live in safety along the Little Tennessee. The Overhill country had been their main center of government and power for as long as the white man had been in America. Its capital city was the beloved town of Chota, where by Cherokee tradition the tribal "mother fire" was kept. The town also served as a place of refuge for those caught up in intratribal violence.

But now Cherokee leaders felt compelled to move to the south, taking with them the seat of Cherokee government and the Cherokee tribal fire. They resettled first at their town of Tellico on the Tellico River. But the continuing press of Anglo-Americans drove them even farther south to a new location at New Echota, Georgia. This constituted the first forced removal of the Cherokees from the heart of their Overhill homeland.

Corn Tassel's murder touched off several more years of bloody warfare on the Tennessee frontier. The Cherokees were led by John Watts. Watts, like the famed inventor of the Cherokee alphabet, Sequoyah (also known as George Guess), was a nephew of Corn Tassel. Watts so loved and admired his uncle that he was known as Young Tassel. During the next four years, Watts sent his Cherokee warriors rampaging against settlements on the Nolichucky, Watauga, Holston, and French Broad rivers of eastern Tennessee. Watts himself was severely wounded in an attack against whites on the Cumberland River near present-day Nashville.

American militia struck back at the Chickamaugan towns, burning Cherokee homes and forcing Watts and other war leaders

New Echota restoration, New Echota, Georgia   *(Photo by Stan Hoig)*

to sue for peace. At a council held at the Tellico Blockhouse in October 1794, the Chickamaugans signed a peace agreement with the United States. One of their chiefs, Bloody Fellow, declared, "I want peace, that we may sleep in our homes."

From that day on, the Cherokee Nation ceased to war with the United States. Though they did not then realize it, their eventual removal from their native homeland had become a virtual certainty.

NOTES

p. 3   "Pangs of parting . . ." Carolyn Thomas Foreman, "The Coodey Family of Indian Territory," *Chronicles of Oklahoma*, 15 (Winter 1947–48): 331, citing Coodey to John Howard Payne, August 13, 1840, Newberry Library, Ayer Collection, "Payne Manuscripts," VI.

p. 3   "a voice of divine indignation . . ." Grant Foreman, *Indian Removal, the Emigration of the Five Civilized Tribes* (Norman: University of Oklahoma Press, 1933), p. 290, citing Coodey to John

Howard Payne, August 13, 1840, Newberry Library, Ayer Collection, "Payne Manuscripts," VI.

p. 6   "The traders . . ." *Colonial Records of South Carolina, Journals of the Commissioners of the Indian Trade, 1710–1718*, W. L. McDowell, ed. (Columbia, S.C.: South Carolina Archives Dept., 1955), p. 442.

p. 6   "I have a hatchet . . ." "A Treaty Between the Catawbas and Cherokees, 1756," *Virginia Magazine of History and Biography*, 13 (January 1906): 251.

p. 7   "All their towns . . ." *Scot's Magazine* (Edinburgh, Scotland), August 1761, p. 430.

p. 9   "I am fond . . ." *American State Papers, Indian Affairs*, II, p. 41.

p. 10   "You have bought . . ." John Brown, "Eastern Cherokee Chiefs," *Chronicles of Oklahoma* 16 (March 1938): 20.

p. 11   "no white man . . ." John Haywood, *The Civil and Political History of the State of Tennessee* (Nashville: House of the Methodist Episcopal Church, South, 1915), p. 502.

p. 11   "It is a little . . ." Sam'l C. Williams, "Tatham's Characters Among the North American Indians," *Tennessee Historical Magazine* 7 (October 1921): p. 176.

p. 13   "They [the chiefs] came . . ." September 18, 1788.

p. 14   "I want peace . . ." John P. Brown, *Old Frontiers, the Story of the Cherokee Indians from Earliest Times to the Date of their Removal to the West, 1838* (Kingsport, Tenn.: Southern Publishers, 1938), p. 440.

Land for Peace

The Cherokees had long been split over how to deal with the whites who pressed against their land, killed their game, and severely altered their lives. By 1800 it had become clear, even to those so inclined, that warring was ineffective and self-destructive. Cherokee warriors could not compete against the might of United States arms. It was impossible to protect their home villages and families from assault. Peaceful leaders clung to the hope that the land cessions of each new treaty would satisfy white demands.

Further, the Cherokees were quickly adapting themselves to the ways of white society. Increasingly the men planted crops, tended livestock, and became involved in trade. The women worked industriously at their spinning wheels and looms. Since 1800, more and more tribespeople had begun listening to the missionaries and taking up Christianity. Some of their young, mostly children of marriages between Cherokee women and white men, were being educated at the missions or even studying at schools in the North.

Other Cherokees, however, sought to escape the onslaught of white influence and disturbance by moving west. A vast wilderness beyond the Mississippi River was as yet unspoiled by white men. Nor was this lost on the federal government. Officials saw a solution to the "Indian problem" of the East by persuading the

Cherokees and other tribes to give up their lands in exchange for those in the Far West.

As early as 1782, a delegation of Cherokees applied to Don Estevan Miro, governor of Spanish-held Louisiana, for permission to settle west of the Mississippi. Just when the first Cherokees migrated there is not certain. Some historians say that it was some time prior to 1790 when a group of tribespeople who were dissatisfied with the Treaty of Hopewell moved to the St. Francis River of southeastern Missouri and founded a settlement.

But reestablishing a permanent life in the West was never easy. Natives of a region always resisted newcomers who intruded into their hunting areas. The St. Francis Cherokees were constantly at war with the Missouri Osages and other tribes. In 1787 a battle with the Sac and Fox Indians on the Merrimac River of Missouri cost the Cherokees twenty-eight men. Over the years, other tribesmen came west to join the St. Francis settlement. One group was a band of Lower Cherokees who fled from Alabama in 1794 following their massacre of a boatload of whites traveling down the Tennessee River.

The United States policy of Indian removal first took shape under the administration of Thomas Jefferson. As a youngster, Jefferson witnessed parties of Indians as they passed his father's Virginia estate to make pilgrimages to the graves of their dead. Later, as a nineteen-year-old student at William and Mary College in 1762, he listened with admiration as Cherokee chief Ostenaco addressed an assembly at Williamsburg's capitol building.

Still, under Jefferson's administration questionable ploys were used to gain Indian land. Government traders were encouraged to keep the Cherokees indebted in order to obtain their land more easily. Officials continued the standard practice of bribing Indian leaders in order to get them to sign away territory through treaties.

In his purchase of the vast Louisiana country, Jefferson was thinking, in part, of the potential it offered of removing Indian tribes from the East. His idea, however, was based on voluntary removal, which was promoted extensively by Return J. Meigs, U.S. agent to the Cherokees. In 1809 Jefferson himself spoke with a Cherokee delegation in Washington. He encouraged the tribe to send an exploring party to investigate the land along the Arkansas and White rivers as a place to live.

The issue of selling Cherokee land was brought to a point of deadly friction by two treaties that the United States made with the Cherokees in 1805 and 1806. In return for land concessions, the United States made secret grants to Chief Doublehead, a leading Chickamaugan Cherokee from the Lower Towns. Doublehead was given a tract ten miles long and ten miles wide at Muscle Shoals along the Tennessee River of northwestern Alabama. The government hoped that he would use the land to establish a Cherokee village that would reflect the living modes of modern civilization.

When other Cherokee leaders learned that Doublehead had leased land to white men, they were furious. They were incensed both that Doublehead had taken what they considered to be a bribe and that he was, as rumor had it, selling land to whites. A secret meeting was held in which it was agreed that Doublehead would be killed.

The deed was carried out on August 7, 1807, when Doublehead came up the Tennessee River to attend the annual Cherokee ball play at Hiwassee town. His principal attacker was a war captain named Ridge. Ridge was assisted by a white trader named John Rogers and by a half-blood Cherokee named Sanders.

One result of Doublehead's land dealings and subsequent assassination was an intense animosity between the chiefs of the Upper and Lower towns. A national council to restore harmony was called at Willstown, Alabama, in September 1809. In order to prevent individuals from dealing in Cherokee lands on their own, a committee of chiefs was chosen to direct the nation's business. However, the Willstown agreement failed to satisfy Chief Tahlonteskee, a brother of Doublehead. He wrote to President Jefferson, announcing his intention to remove west of the Mississippi River: "I and my party are determined to cross the river towards the West. Our bad brothers may dispute, but with me 12 towns go."

In July 1809, Tahlonteskee and seventeen of his warriors came upriver. They presented agent Return J. Meigs with a list of 1,023 of the Lower Town people who wanted to move west of the Mississippi. On the list were 386 men and 637 women and children. Other Cherokees under Sanlowee and Bowle joined the group, adding 63 more people. Meigs's support of the Cherokees consisted of providing each man with a rifle and a blanket.

The Tahlonteskee group took with them 1,273 black cattle, 369 horses, 868 hogs, 46 spinning wheels, 13 looms, and 36 plows. The removal was made by flatboat and canoe down the Tennessee, Ohio, and Mississippi rivers. Much of the Cherokees' livestock was driven directly overland.

Some of the more well-to-do Cherokees had long since taken up the Southern practice of owning slaves, and included in Tahlonteskee's party were 68 black people. These and numerous other blacks have long been overlooked as participants in the great removals of the Indian tribes of the South.

The journey was not without danger and hardships. On June 23, 1810, Tahlonteskee—through the help of his aide, John D. Chisholm—wrote to Meigs that three of his people had been killed by Choctaw Indians. A year later he reported from the St. Francis settlement saying that he and his people were tired of living in camps. He wanted to exchange his Alabama portion of the Cherokee Nation for lands on the Arkansas River where he and his people could settle down permanently, start farms, and build houses to live in.

From this first removal under the auspices of the United States sprang a sizable Cherokee entity in Arkansas. Soon they had established homes and communities along the north bank of the Arkansas River west of Little Rock at sites known as Remove, Illinois Bayou, Pine Bayou, Spadra Bluffs, Horsehead, Frog, and Mulberry. The group under Bowle founded a Cherokee settlement on the Jean Petite River south of the Arkansas.

Moving west with the Cherokees was Walter Webber, son of the red-headed Will Webber, founder of Willstown. The younger Webber opened a store at the mouth of Illinois Bayou in Arkansas.

Willstown Mission marker, Fort Payne, Alabama. *(Photo by Stan Hoig)*

In 1813 the Cherokees were joined by William Lovely, who was detached from Hiwassee Garrison as their government subagent.

Tahlonteskee's Cherokees proved to be determined and industrious. They built log cabin homes, cleared patches of land for planting vegetable gardens and crops, and erected rail fences to control their horses, cattle, and hogs. The men supported their farming efforts by trading pelts and meat of the deer, bear, and other animals they hunted among the forested hills along the Arkansas. In return, traders brought salt, sugar, whiskey, and other items to them from Arkansas Post at the juncture of the Arkansas, White, and Mississippi rivers.

One of the main arguments for moving west that had been made by President Jefferson and other government officials was that it would allow the Indians to escape from the white man. But the Cherokees soon found there was no such relief in Arkansas. Frontier whites who had filtered into the region were soon complaining about the "barbarous" newcomers. They charged that the Cherokees had murdered a white man and disemboweled his corpse. When white citizens petitioned to the government for relief and protection, Subagent Lovely responded by defining an area for the Cherokees north of the Arkansas River. Arkansas whites then complained that the Cherokees had been given the best and richest land.

The Cherokees on the Jean Petite south of the Arkansas became disturbed by the continued pressure of white civilization. They were determined to search farther to the southwest for a place where there were no white people. Led by Chief Bowle and half-blood Richard Fields, they settled temporarily just north of the Red River near present-day Texarkana, Texas. After a time they moved on west and took up permanent residence in what was then the Mexican province of Texas.

Again, as on the St. Francis, the Arkansas Cherokees were forced to defend their right of possession against the Osages. Horse thievery, warring, and murder continued unabated between the two tribes. Of particular concern to Tahlonteskee's band was the Osage band under Chief Clermont, whose village was located to their west on the Verdigris River of what is now northeastern Oklahoma. Clermont's warriors stood between Arkansas and the buffalo prairie—"a barrier to the setting sun," the Cherokees said.

The intertribal warring came to a head in 1817 when the Cherokees launched a well-planned attack on Clermont's village. They were supported by other enemies of the Osages and by

HEROES OF HORSESHOE BEND

On March 27, 1814, Andrew Jackson's army of East Tennessee militia and Indians attacked and defeated a fortified encampment of rebellious Creek Red Stick warriors at Horseshoe Bend on the Tallapoosa River in Alabama. A year earlier the Red Sticks had massacred some 500 people at Fort Mims, Alabama. Though only a minor engagement compared to many, Horseshoe Bend may have been one of America's most significant battles. Jackson's victory there and soon after at New Orleans launched him on the road to the presidency of the United States.

For the Cherokees, who played a major role in the fight, it was a matter of personal heroics and tribal pride. In earlier times they had warred with enemy tribes, and for a while they had attempted to resist white intrusion onto their lands by force of arms. By the 1790s, however, even the war leaders had realized that the military might of the United States was too overwhelming. But the ethic of warriorship was still strong with the Cherokees. When General James White and his Tennessee militia arrived at Hiwassee Garrison on their way to the Creek country in October 1813, the Cherokees offered their help.

One of them was a smallish young Cherokee whose bloodlines were predominantly Scottish. His name was John Ross. Another was a middle-aged Cherokee who walked with a limp. This man, a lowly private who wore the turban, leggings, and moccasins of an old-style tribesman, was called Sequoyah. With the militia was a white man who had lived among the Cherokees as a boy. His name was Sam Houston.

The Cherokees dressed their heads with white feathers and deer tails to distinguish themselves from the Creeks in battle. Some were on foot and some, like Sequoyah, rode their own mounts. Their arms were a mixture of muskets, rifles, swords, tomahawks, lances, bows and arrows, and knives. Once organized, they eagerly fell in behind as the militiamen, decked in coonskin caps and buckskins, marched off down the Tennessee River.

The Cherokees missed the action when Davy Crockett and other Tennesseans defeated the Creeks at Talleschatchee on November 4. However, they were in on the November 18 burning and sacking of the Creek village of Hillabee. Sixty-one Creeks were killed there, and 250 others taken prisoner.

After this engagement, the Cherokees returned home while more Tennessee militia were being recruited. But in February of 1814 the tribesmen were reenlisted and once again marched south to Turkeytown in Alabama, where Fort Armstrong was being constructed on the Coosa River. From there Jackson led his militia and their Cherokee allies through thick forest and marshlands to where six Creek towns were fortified behind log breastworks inside a horseshoe bend of the Tallapoosa.

Jackson deployed the Cherokees to the east side of the river to cut off any Creek retreat while he attacked with his militia and his two small cannons. Neither the artillery nor attacks by the militia were effective, and Jackson appeared to be stymied.

The Cherokee warriors, however, were impatient to be in the fight. Three of them jumped in the river and swam to where Creek canoes lined the opposite bank. Pushing a canoe before them, they took the boat back to their lines. Other Cherokees jumped into the canoe and, under heavy fire, crossed the river and captured the remaining canoes. The Cherokees then engaged the Creeks in a fierce battle, drawing them off and permitting Jackson's militiamen to overrun the Creek ramparts.

The Red Sticks were overwhelmed in a bloody skirmish. A battlefield count revealed 557 Creek dead, while many others were believed to have drowned in the river while trying to escape. The Cherokees suffered the highest casualty rate among Jackson's army. They were lauded highly for their bravery and for the key role they played, but this did not stop the militiamen from seizing Cherokee cattle and pigs to eat on their way home. Nor did it deter Andrew Jackson from doing all in his power as president to remove the Cherokees from their beloved homeland.

Cherokee warriors who came from the Old Nation (Cherokee Nation in the South) to help. Some of the latter had fought with General Jackson against the Creeks in the Battle of Horseshoe Bend in 1814. Striking the Osage village while Clermont and his warriors were away on a buffalo hunt, the Cherokees burned the village and its food supply, massacred most of its inhabitants, and took Osage women and children captives.

Despite their conflicts and difficulties, the Arkansas Cherokees made significant progress toward establishing a stable society. They formalized a government, created a light horse police force, and supported schooling for their children. Their advancement was furthered by the arrival of a government trade factory, the opening of a cotton gin, and the establishment of Dwight Mission on the west bank of Illinois Bayou. The bloody war with the Osages would continue on well into the 1820s, though it was held in check by two new military posts on the Arkansas River, Fort Smith and Fort Gibson.

Other Cherokees began to migrate in from the Old Nation. Chickamaugan chiefs such as Toochelar and Dick Justice brought their families west. The old warrior chief Takatoka arrived in 1813 and quickly assumed a leading role in the Osage war and in efforts to form an alliance of western tribes.

The migrations continued under pressure from the administration of James Monroe (1817–25), which formulated a plan for exiling Eastern Indian tribes to the trans-Mississippi West. Key efforts to remove the Cherokees were made through treaties in 1817 and 1819. In these pacts, the Cherokees ceded all their lands north of Tennessee's Hiwassee River. To any Cherokee wishing to exchange his lands for those in Arkansas, the government less than generously offered one rifle and ammunition, one blanket, one brass kettle, and one beaver trap.

In 1818 a large contingent of Cherokees under Chief John Jolly from the Hiwassee arrived and settled near Spadra Bluffs. With them came the old trader John Rogers and his four part-Cherokee sons, all of whom ultimately played major roles in the affairs of the Western Cherokees. After Tahlonteskee died in 1819, the rotund, likable Jolly became the principal chief.

There were also smaller, independent migrations, such as that of Sequoyah (George Guess), who migrated from Willstown with four other families in 1824. His wife Sally Guess later said in a

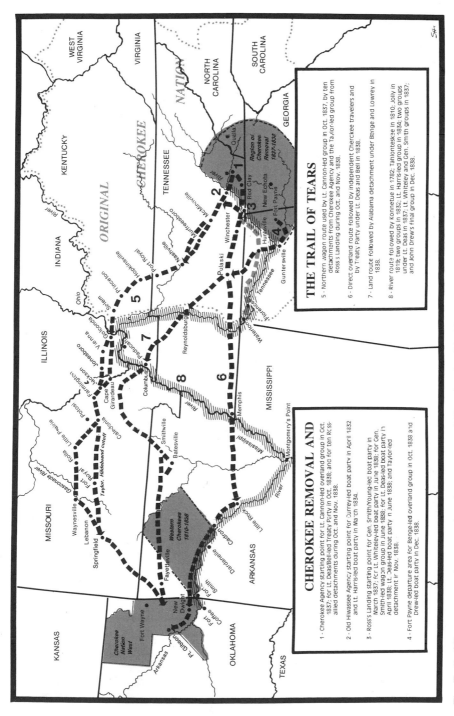

THE TRAIL OF TEARS

5 - Northern wagon route used by Lt. Cannon-led group in Oct. 1837, by ten detachments from Cherokee Agency and the Taylor-led group from Ross's Landing during Oct. and Nov. 1838.

6 - Direct overland route followed by independent Cherokee travelers and by Treaty Party under Lt. Deas and Bell in 1838.

7 - Land route followed by Alabama detachment under Benge and Lowrey in 1838.

8 - River route followed by Konnetue in 1782; Tahlonteskie in 1810; Jolly in 1819; two groups in 1832; Lt. Harris-led group in 1834; two groups under Lt. Deas in 1837; Lt. Whiteley and Gen. Smith groups in 1837; and John Drew's final group in Dec. 1838.

CHEROKEE REMOVAL AND

1 - Cherokee Agency starting point for Lt. Cannon-led overland group in Oct. 1837; for Lt. Deas/Bell-led Treaty Party in Oct. 1838; and for ten Ross-allied detachments during Oct. and Nov. 1838.

2 - Old Hiwassee Agency starting point for Currey-led boat party in April 1832 and Lt. Harris-led boat party in March 1834.

3 - Ross's Landing starting point for Gen. Smith/Young-led boat party in March 1837; for Lt. Whiteley-led boat party in June 1838; for Gen. Smith-led wagon group in June 1838; for Lt. Deas-led boat party in April 1838; Lt. Deas-led boat party in June 1838; and Taylor-led detachment in Nov. 1838.

4 - Fort Payne departure area for Benge-led overland group in Oct. 1838 and Drew-led boat party in Dec. 1838.

The Trail of Tears: removal area, emigration routes, and Cherokee land holdings.   *(Map by Stan Hoig)*

claims affidavit: "There was only five families came on to this country at that time. We had no wagon . . . packed our things on horses."

The Guesses established their new home on the Illinois Bayou about fifteen miles from its mouth. It was well away from the white people whom they, too, wished to avoid. The inventor of the Cherokee syllabary (see box feature, p. 31) was a highly respected figure of his day. Though he sought no office among his people, he was at times called on to take part in important tribal matters.

In 1828 Sequoyah was appointed a member of a delegation to go to Washington, D.C. to arrange for a legal survey of the Cherokees' Arkansas lands. Reacting to pleas from whites in Arkansas, however, government officials were determined to initiate a new treaty with the Western Cherokees.

They demanded that the Cherokees exchange their holdings in Arkansas for a body of land farther west that had earlier been purchased from the Osages by Subagent Lovely. Sequoyah's delegation had no authority to make such a pact. However, the members were held in their Washington hotel virtually as captives and cajoled until finally they gave in and signed the treaty.

By the Treaty of 1828, the Western Cherokees were again uprooted from their homes. They were now forced to move, without help from the government, up the Arkansas River to what is now northeastern Oklahoma. Agent Edward DuVal pointed out to Secretary of War James Barbour what it entailed for the Cherokees. They would, he noted, be forced to leave their fields and improvements on which they had toiled for years. They would lose at least one year's crop, and endure great hardship and suffering in resettling in a remote area away from the conveniences they then knew.

Peace with the Osages finally came, and the Cherokees set about reestablishing their lives along the Arkansas River west of Fort Smith. Migrations of tribespeople from the Old Nation continued. In 1829 the Westerners were joined by an old acquaintance who had lived among them for a time as a boy. This

ELIAS BOUDINOT, CHEROKEE INDIAN LEADER

Cherokee intellectual Elias Boudinot, editor of the *Cherokee Phoenix,* died as a result of his role in the Cherokee removal.   *(Archives & Manuscripts, Oklahoma Historical Society)*

was Sam Houston, only recently resigned as governor of Tennessee following an ill-fated marriage. Houston was adopted as a son by Chief Jolly, an old friend from his boyhood days in Tennessee.

The establishment of a large Cherokee entity in the West had great significance. In the coming years it would offer a potential sanctuary to disgruntled Cherokees from the Old Nation. Educated tribesman Elias Boudinot, promoting the cause of removal, would argue: "We know of none to which the Cherokees can go as an asylum, but that possessed by our brethren west of the Mississippi."

Despite the distance, there was constant contact between the Old Nation and the Western Cherokees, and often relatives were persuaded to move west. Even more important, the government saw in the Western Cherokees an example for removing other Indians from the East. In 1824, Congress accepted the concept of an "Indian Territory" beyond the Mississippi. It was to be a place in which the eastern tribes could be relocated out of the way of national progress.

In the face of persistent government persuasion and pressure, the will to resist removal began to erode among some of the Old Nation tribespeople. In less than thirty years, Tahlonteskee's move west in 1810 would prove to have been a fateful precedent for Cherokees of the Old Nation.

NOTES

p. 18   "I and my party . . ." Turtle at Home, Tolluntuskee, and Glass to Jefferson, November 25, 1808, Records of the First Board of Cherokee Commissioners, M-222, NA.

p. 26   "There was only . . ." Sally Guess affidavit, *1842 Cherokee Claims,* Skin Bayou District, Marybelle W. Chase, comp., 1988, pp. 217–19 (originals located at Tennessee State Library and Archives, Nashville, Tenn.).

p. 28   "We know of none . . ." *House Exec. Doc. No. 91,* 23rd Cong., 2d sess., p. 9.

A Nation, or Not

Teesee Guess was a son of Sequoyah. He had moved to Will's Valley, Alabama, with his parents. The family had been forced to leave their home at Tuskegee on the Little Tennessee by the Treaty of 1819 with the United States. When Sequoyah migrated to the Arkansas country, Teesee remained behind with his wife and two children. He farmed forty acres of partially cleared land, most of which he had enclosed with a rail fence. He and his family lived in a well-finished, hewn-log cabin with a plank floor and clapboard roof. There were also another log cabin, a smokehouse, a springhouse, corn cribs, stables, a horse lot, peach and apple trees, and a garden.

Teesee, his wife Ah-gah-te-yah, and their two children were working in the field one afternoon in 1834 when smoke was seen billowing skyward in the direction of their house. Teesee dashed for home, his family following. But they were too late. Smoke idled skyward from the smoldering ash and charcoal where their cabins and other structures had stood. They had lost all they owned: home, cookhouse, clothing, feather beds, dishes, bowls, quilts, coverlets, utensils, weaving loom, saddles—everything.

Sometime later Teesee discovered that a neighbor, a white man named Mullins, possessed some pot hooks and an iron pot that had been in his house. There was nothing that Teesee could do even though he was fully convinced that Mullins had taken most

Cherokee Phoenix office restoration, New Echota, Georgia.   *(Photo by Stan Hoig)*

of his furniture and other goods in the house before setting it ablaze. An Indian's word against a white man's was of no value in an Alabama court. Mullins, like other white men, considered Indians to have no rights to land or property, and he was supported by the laws of the day. Eventually Teesee was forced to emigrate west. He did so in November 1837.

His loss of home and property was all too typical of other Cherokees who had taken up white ways only to be victimized by the white majority of the day. The Cherokees' condition was a result of measures passed by the United States and the Southern states. The laws were designed to force the Indians to abandon their homeland and remove to the Indian Territory.

In 1827 the Old Nation Cherokees had formed their government under a constitution modeled after that of the United States. It was composed of two houses of congress, a chief executive, and a supreme court. They also established a printing press at their New Echota, Georgia, site. The press used type cast in the Cherokee alphabet invented by Sequoyah. On February 1, 1828, they

SEQUOYAH'S IDEA

In the year 1820 a small group of men was visiting in the home of Cherokee Archibald Campbell at Sauta on the Tennessee River in northern Alabama. One of them was the educated young convert David Brown. Brown had just returned from Knoxville, where he and missionary Daniel Butrick had gone to arrange for publication of a Cherokee spelling book —a translation of Cherokee words into English.

Sequoyah (George Guess) was a member of the Western Cherokees, having moved to Arkansas on his own in 1824. *(Archives & Manuscripts, Oklahoma Historical Society)*

The men were discussing the ability of white men to write their talk on paper and send it far away for others to read and understand almost as if they were face to face. They were all awed and unable to explain just how this mysterious thing could be done. A Cherokee man lounging to one side had been listening to the conversation. He had once been married to Archibald Campbell's sister. His English name was George Guess, but other Cherokees knew him as Sequoyah.

"You are all fools, he said. "Why, the thing is very easy; I can do it myself."

Picking up a flat stone, he began scratching on it with a pin. After drawing a horse and several other images, he read a sentence from them. The others looked at him for a moment, then they all laughed scoffingly and ended their conversation.

But the matter did not end with Sequoyah. He could not stop thinking that it was just as possible for a Cherokee to write his language as a white man. All that was needed was a set of symbols to convey meaning. The more he thought about it the more he was certain it could be done.

When he was back at his home in Wills Valley (now Fort Payne, Alabama), Sequoyah went to the mission store and bought some ink and paper. He made his own pen from a turkey quill. It took him a while before he realized that the end had to be split in order to work well.

He began drawing pictures to represent objects: horses, cows, trees, leaves . . . but there were just too many things. He realized that he would have to try a new approach, one in which symbols would represent vocal sounds. He decided to use the white man's writing as a model. He began modifying English-language letters to use to represent words in the Cherokee tongue. But again there were far too many—hundreds of words. Finally, he saw the answer. His symbols would have to represent syllables that could be put together in various ways to express different ideas.

All this time he had let his work go. People were saying that he was lazy. Some thought that he was in league with the shee-lahs (witches) and practicing evil magic. His wife Sally became so upset with him that once she burned the cabin he had built to work in. Only his six-year-old daughter Ahyokah continued to help him. With her assistance he finally cut the number of characters down to eighty-six.

Now it worked! By using the new Cherokee alphabet that he had created, he could write messages that Ahyokah could read aloud in the Cherokee tongue. But who would believe him? In order to prove the worth of his invention, Sequoyah made a trip to far-off Arkansas in 1821, where other Cherokees had gone to live. There he had a headman write a letter —unseen by Sequoyah—back to a chief in the Old Nation at Willstown.

The letter was sealed with wax, but when it was delivered and opened both Sequoyah and Ahyokah read the message aloud. The listeners were astounded, but they had heard it with their own ears. Sequoyah had given the Cherokees a way to write and read their own language just the same as the white man did! They did not realize it then, but by inventing a complete syllabary, Sequoyah had done something that no other one person in the history of humankind had ever done.

published the first issue of the *Cherokee Phoenix*, the first native language newspaper in America. Cherokee Council also planned to create a national library and a national academy at New Echota.

All of these were remarkable achievements, yet they worked to the political disadvantage of the Cherokees. The creation of a Cherokee republic and its developing societal structures posed a threat to the authority of states such as Georgia. In 1802 Georgia had ceded its western land holdings, those now comprising the states of Alabama and Mississippi, to the United States. In turn the federal government had promised to extinguish all Indian title to land within Georgia. This was to be done as soon as it could be achieved peacefully and at a reasonable cost.

Purchase of the Louisiana territory by the United States, Georgia argued, made that possible. State officials were not at all concerned that in order to carry out this agreement the United States would be required to break solemn treaties that it had made with the Indian tribes who were the original occupants.

Cherokee Old Nation Courthouse, New Echota, Georgia.   *(Photo by Stan Hoig)*

Public clamor against the Indians was only made worse when in July 1829 gold was found on Cherokee land in northern Georgia. The discovery soon proved to be disastrous for them. It not only excited gold fever among whites but whetted the desire of

Georgians to rid themselves of the Cherokees altogether. In response, the Georgia legislature immediately passed a series of anti-Indian laws.

These measures stripped the Cherokees of their land in Georgia and denied them even the right of protest by law. It was made illegal for a Cherokee to testify against a white man in court. Cherokee Nation laws were voided. Contracts between an Indian and a white man were invalid unless witnessed by two whites. It was declared to be against the law for any Cherokee to dissuade another Cherokee from emigrating west. It was illegal for an Indian to hire a white man.

As a result of the discovery of gold on Cherokee land, the Georgia legislature created Cherokee County out of the area and subdivided it into land lots and gold lots. These lots were then offered to white citizens in a state-operated lottery. Indians were prohibited from digging gold, though whites could.

Even as white gold-seekers flooded into the region, the Cherokees were driven out by soldiers of the newly formed Georgia Guard. The Indians were often prodded with bayonets or struck with rifle butts. Alabama soon adopted many of the same restrictive laws as Georgia had.

Teesee was by no means the only one to suffer. The tales of white atrocities later told by the Cherokees were endless. In a claim affidavit, Cloy-yah-cah testified that he had resisted a man who kept intruding on his property and trying to take it over. One day while he and his wife were away, the house was set on fire and burned down with everything in it. Another Cherokee called Young Chicken claimed that once when he went into a store at a settlement, a man climbed on his horse and rode off with it. Young Chicken never saw his horse or saddle again. A tribesman named Bread was panning for gold in a stream when he was seized, beaten, and sent to prison. After being run off his property by whites, Cherokee Alfred Denton went to enroll for removal. When he returned to get his stock, he was again run off, this time by government agents.

Tribesman Richard Saunders said that whites forced him to live in the woods for two years before he finally migrated. Jim Downing was driven out of his home and property six years before he started west. Adam Bible had planted a crop near Nickajack on

This Napoleonic miniature was made of Andrew Jackson only a year after the Battle of Horseshoe Bend. He was 48 at the time. *(Library of Congress)*

the Tennessee River. While he was gone one day, his rail fence was set on fire and his entire 80 acres of crops destroyed. He went to officials to complain, and he himself was jailed. Another man, Tay-kah-huttah, claimed that he was falsely charged with assault, whereupon he was arrested, severely beaten, and imprisoned for six weeks. During that time a white man took over his property.

Andrew Jackson, elected president in 1828, was an avid supporter of the rights of the Southern states. Despite the military help the Cherokees had given him, Jackson had the same attitude toward Native Americans that was common among frontier whites. He insisted that Indians "have neither the intelligence, the industry, the moral habits nor the desire of improvement which are essential to any favorable change in their condition."

In his first address to Congress, on December 8, 1829, Jackson avowed his determination to remove the Indians. He initiated a bill for relocating all the eastern tribes to lands west of the Mississippi River. The Indian Removal Bill was argued in Congress during April and May, 1830.

The debate was based on the issue of whether or not the Cherokees deserved the status of autonomy. Senator Theodore Frelinghuysen of New Jersey, responding to the complaint by Georgia that the United States was encroaching on its sovereignty, proclaimed: "Sir, the Cherokees are no parties to this issue; they have no concern in this controversy. They hold by better title than either Georgia or the Union."

He also pointed to the several treaties made between the United States and the Cherokees. By these agreements, the Cherokees were placed under the protection of the United States and assigned specific territorial boundaries. The issue of the Georgia anti-Indian laws was also considered at great length. Speaking before the U.S. House, Representative John Test of Indiana observed: "Why, Sir, the whites may go into their towns, and murder men, women and children with perfect impunity, unless, indeed, there should happen to be an honest white man present, which will hardly ever be the case."

Andrew Jackson as President. The Cherokees helped make a national hero of Jackson only to have him become the most relentless proponent of their removal west.   (Illustrated London News, *July 12, 1845)*

Senator Edward Everett of Massachusetts stated the Cherokees' plight even more emphatically. "When I am asked, then, what the Cherokee has to fear from the law of Georgia, I answer, that, by law, he is left at the mercy of the firebrand and dagger of every unprincipled wretch in the country."

Georgia defended its actions by insisting that the Cherokees, having sided with England in the Revolutionary War, were a conquered people. It was charged that the United States had no right to overrule Georgia in regard to the treatment of its own population. The state, it was argued, was not liable for previous compacts, called treaties, that had been made by the federal government. Further, it was wrong for an independent state to be limited by the presence of a tribe of "savages."

Jackson's Indian Removal Bill barely passed in the House of Representatives by a five-vote margin, and passed in the Senate by about the same amount. During its January 1831 term, the U.S. Supreme Court heard arguments in a suit brought by the Cherokee Nation against the State of Georgia. The Cherokees sought an injunction to protect them against the unjust Georgia laws.

Chief Justice John Marshall rendered the majority opinion denying the injunction. He concluded that, even though great wrongs may have been inflicted, the Court did not have the right to control the Georgia legislature. Associate Justice Smith Thompson offered the dissenting opinion. He contended that the injunction should be awarded "under the laws of the United States, and treaties made under their authority with the Cherokee Nation, and which laws and treaties have been and are threatened to be still further violated by the laws of the State of Georgia."

Marshall essentially reversed this *Cherokees v. Georgia* opinion in the case of Cherokee George Tassel, who was executed in Georgia despite a federal writ of delay. Marshall now held that in Indian matters, the laws of Georgia were inferior to those of the United States.

In the fall of 1831, Jackson established the position of superintendent of Indian removal and appointed an old friend, former congressman Benjamin Currey, to the post. Currey's job was to actively recruit Cherokees for removal. He would soon prove willing to use virtually any means necessary to do so.

The Cherokees had their own public supporters. Among them were William Wirt, a former U.S. attorney general; the outspoken Senator Daniel Webster; and Boston's Jeremiah Evarts, a founder of the American Board of Commissioners for Foreign Missions. Additionally, the *Cherokee Phoenix* newspaper, which effectively argued the Cherokee position, was reprinted in other newspapers, and many pro-Cherokee editorials were used in sermons by ministers. Georgia proponents denigrated such Cherokee backing as "the work of fanatics, and pretended philanthropists, who had their own purposes to answer, and who were well paid for their services from the Cherokee treasury."

Actually the treatment received by Teesee Guess was much the same as that accorded to many Cherokees in Georgia. Sometimes a tribesman would be served whiskey by whites, who would then have the Indian arrested for drunkenness by the Georgia Guard. The white citizens would then rush forward to grab the Indian's property.

Chief John Ross himself returned from Washington, D.C. in April 1833 to discover that his home and plantation had been invaded and taken over by lottery winners. He entered his house at night only to find that it was in the possession of strangers. His family was gone; he knew not where. Indeed, the new tenants permitted him to stay the night only if he paid for the privilege.

The next morning he rose at daybreak and looked about the yards that had once been his. Cattle and sheep browsed untended, and his cornfield stood unharvested. His flock of peacocks roosted in the majestic oak overlooking the graveyard where his father and one of his children were buried. Ross paid his bill and rode off to search for his wife Quatie, who had been ill, and their two children. He finally found them struggling along a road to Tennessee in a heavy rainstorm.

The Rosses relocated in a one-room cabin just north of the Georgia-Tennessee line. Ross and the Cherokee Council reestablished their Nation's capital at a nearby site in Tennessee known as Red Clay. The state line, however, would fail to deter the Georgia Guard from intimidating the Indians.

Missionary Samuel Worcester, who was imprisoned in Georgia for his loyalty to the Cherokees, moved west with them to present-day Oklahoma. *(Archives & Manuscripts, Oklahoma Historical Society)*

Georgia also moved to nullify the influence of the missionaries among the Cherokees, passing a law that required the churchmen to take an oath of allegiance to the state. Eleven of them were arrested. Nine of these either signed the oath or left the state. But two, Samuel Worcester and Elizur Butler, refused to do either. Accordingly, they were sentenced to four years in prison. They were incarcerated along with common criminals in cotton shirts and trousers bearing their initials and length of sentence.

Georgia was not alone in its unrelenting determination to drive the Cherokees west. Andrew Jackson had his own plans for removing the Indians—the tried and true practice of treaty by bribery. "Nothing is more certain," another senator observed, "than that, if the chiefs and influential men could be brought into the measure, the rest would implicitly follow."

The Indian Removal Act did not call for the use of force to remove the Indians. However, it and public sentiment provided Jackson with the opportunity of withdrawing federal protection for the Indians and supporting the demands of states' rights in the matter. Moreover, he launched a new treaty-making scheme for the purpose of procuring, by any means, the title to the lands of the Cherokees and other Southern tribes.

Still, probably no one, not even Jackson himself, realized the severe consequences that the tactics of the government would wreak among the Cherokees. Adding to the loss of their tribal homeland were seething intratribal feuds that the volatile issue of removal had spawned within the Cherokee Nation itself.

NOTES

p. 32   "You are all . . ." *Daily National Intelligencer,* September 16, 1828. See also Stan Hoig, *Sequoyah, the Cherokee Genius* (Oklahoma City: Oklahoma Historical Society, 1995), pp. 31–42.

p. 37   "have neither . . ." William G. McLoughlin, *Cherokees and Missionaries, 1789-1839* (New Haven: Yale University Press, 1984), p. 15.

p. 37   "Sir, the Cherokees . . ." *U.S. Register of Debates,* Reel 2, p. 312.

p. 37   "Why, Sir . . ." *Speeches on the Passage of the Bill for the Removal of the Indians Delivered in Congress of the United States April and May, 1830* (Boston: Perkins and Marvin, 1830), p. 304.

p. 38   "When I am asked . . ." *Speeches on the Passage,* p. 263.

p. 39   "under the laws . . ." Cherokee Nation *v.* Georgia, *Decisions of the Supreme Court of the United States, Lawyers Edition,* Book 8 (1831), US 30–33, pp. 32, 53.

p. 40   "the work of fanatics . . ." *Speeches on the Passage,* p. viii.

p. 42   "Nothing is . . ." *U.S. Register of Debates,* Reel 2, p. 312.

The Treaty of New Echota

In October 1835, John Howard Payne, noted playwright and the author of the song "Home, Sweet Home," was a guest in the log cabin home of John Ross near present-day Chattanooga. As such, he became witness to a unique procession of Cherokees who passed by on their way to the Red Clay meeting grounds. By agreement, the Cherokee national council was to meet there to consider a treaty that was being offered by Andrew Jackson's emissary. With great sympathy and admiration, Payne observed the tribespeople as they emerged in long lines from the fall-tinted woods and stopped by to pay homage to Ross. Most were on foot, but some of the old ones rode on horseback. Ross met them at his gate. The Indians formed two lines and came forward to shake his hand solemnly and respectfully.

These were traditional Cherokees. Many still wore the colorful turban, tunic, or long robe, and sash of the old-style tribesman. They carried their own blankets, rolled up and thrown over the shoulder, a tin cup, and—some of them—a pan for cooking on the trail. Some had walked up to sixty miles since the day before and were very tired. After taking water from Ross's well, they rested. They seated themselves on logs, on the rail fence that enclosed Ross's log cabin, or sat cross-legged under trees. The older men

John Howard Payne, famous as a playwright and author of the song "Home Sweet Home," was a faithful friend of the Cherokees. *(Archives & Manuscripts, Oklahoma Historical Society)*

remained near Ross, asking about the upcoming meeting and how to reach Red Clay.

After a time, they were called together in assembly around Ross as the chief informed them of his wishes concerning Jackson's treaty. Presently an elder gave a command, and the tribespeople once again took up their goods and fell in line toward Red Clay.

In seeking to remove the Cherokees, there were two factors that Andrew Jackson had not counted on. These were the stubborn resistance of John Ross and the strong following he had among the Cherokee people. Ross would prove to be a painful thorn in the president's side and a shrewd political adversary.

When Jackson had invited the Cherokees to meet him at Nashville in August 1830 to discuss the terms of a new treaty, Ross and other leaders had refused to attend. The wisdom of this became all too apparent in September at Dancing Rabbit Creek, Mississippi. There Jackson's commissioners bribed three Choctaw chiefs, getting them to sign a removal treaty that ceded away all of the Choctaw lands in the South. Soon after that, the Chickasaws, Creeks, and Seminoles followed. The Cherokee leaders now saw their nation as a "solitary tree in an open space where all the trees around have been prostrated by a furious tornado—save one."

The State of Georgia's determination to rid itself of its Indian population was expressed by Wilson Lumpkin, formerly a Georgia governor and at that time a U. S. senator, in addressing the U.S. Congress:

> If we determine upon their emigration to the West, the sooner they know it, the better. That they may send their Calebs and Joshuas to search out and view the promised land, for situated *as they now are, and where they are*, there is no rest for the sole of an Indian boot.

The Cherokee national council made a plea to Jackson to continue the federal protection promised by treaties. Instead, the president ordered that the annual $6,000 annuity payments, owed the Cherokees for past land cessions, be made directly to individual Cherokees rather than through the Cherokee government. In response, the Cherokee legislature gave John Ross the power to employ William Wirt as legal counsel. Also lending their support were such men as Jeremiah Evarts and Daniel Webster. However, deprived of the treaty revenue, Ross and his followers had little money with which to fight their legal battles with Georgia and the Jackson administration.

Now Ross was faced with another severe problem—that of internal dissension among the Cherokees themselves over the issue of making a new treaty with the government. Jackson and the State of Georgia had managed to agitate the long-standing split among the Cherokees over removal. There were tribespeople who wanted to escape the oppression and misery they suffered or simply desired to get away from the white people around them. Others were intimidated or lured by false promises into signing up for removal.

The large majority of Cherokees, though, stood with Ross—through intimidation, Currey and others claimed. The most serious threat to Ross's leadership came from some of the most prominent figures of the Cherokee Nation. Among them were Major Ridge, the assassin of Doublehead; his formally educated son, John Ridge; Elias Boudinot, the capable editor of the *Cherokee Phoenix;* and Ross's own brother, Andrew.

At the beginning of the Cherokee contest with Jackson and Georgia, these men had been stout supporters of resisting removal. But in the fall of 1832, a change of thinking began to surface among them. As president of the Cherokee national council, John Ridge proposed sending a delegation to Washington for the pur-

Major Ridge's home, Rome, Georgia. *(Photo by Stan Hoig)*

pose of discussing a removal treaty. Ross beat down this effort and in the spring of 1833 put himself at the head of a delegation to the capital. While there, he rejected a Jackson offer of $3 million for the Cherokee lands in Tennessee, Alabama, and Georgia. The Cherokee gold mines alone were worth that, Ross argued.

When Ross demanded that nothing that encouraged removal be printed in the *Cherokee Phoenix*, Boudinot resigned as editor. Ross appointed Elijah Hicks to replace him. Boudinot, who had worked very hard to recruit funds for the Cherokee press and to cast a typeface in the Sequoyan syllabary, was deeply incensed over the matter. The *Phoenix* finally ceased publication in the spring of 1834.

During Ross's absence from home, however, U.S. and Georgia agents had managed a secret alliance with the pro-removal faction. Only after the removal did it become known that the properties of the two Ridges, of Boudinot, and of certain other pro-removal Cherokees had been exempted from lottery takeover by Georgia authorities. The homes of these men were left virtually untouched even as those of Ross, the wealthy Joseph Vann, George Lowrey, Elijah Hicks, and others were invaded and taken over violently by Georgia citizens.

In a November 1834 meeting at the home of John Ridge, with Ben Currey present, the members of the pro-removal faction openly organized themselves as the Cherokee Treaty party. Their avowed purpose was to displace John Ross as the Cherokee principal chief. The Jackson administration offered to put up $3,000 in expense money for their delegation to visit Washington.

Jackson received them warmly while ignoring John Ross, who skillfully worked to gain the support of Congress for his own National party. Finally Ross was given an audience with the president. Jackson offered first $3,250,000, then $4,500,000 for the Cherokee lands. Ross demanded $20,000,000, creating a standoff. Jackson accused him of stalling in an effort to delay and prevent removal—an accusation that was altogether true.

Disregarding Ross, the Jackson administration and the Treaty party agreed on the $4,500,000 figure. The approval of the Chero-

Rich Joe Vann, one of the wealthiest of Cherokees, lost his entire estate in the Georgia land lottery.   *(Archives & Manuscripts, Oklahoma Historical Society)*

kee people was to be secured, if possible, prior to the forthcoming presidential election. To that purpose, Jackson appointed the Reverend John F. Schermerhorn as a special commissioner to the Cherokees and sent him with the treaty delegation to New Echota in the spring of 1835. Arrival of the Dutch Presbyterian minister reflected a prediction that one Cherokee had made earlier.

"I reckon now," the tribesman had wryly observed, "General Jackson will send one of his biggest liars."

On the night of March 29, Schermerhorn and more than a dozen of the Treaty men met in secret at the home of Elias Boudinot. By flickering candlelight, they signed a pact agreeing to the sale of the Old Nation homeland and tribal removal to the Indian Territory. Schermerhorn remained in Cherokee country for the rest of the year, working to influence the Cherokee people to accept removal.

When Schermerhorn presented a plan to make a distribution of the Cherokees' annuity outside of Ross's jurisdiction, the chief persuaded his people to vote against it. Further, they refused to have anything to do with Schermerhorn, whom they called Skaynooyaynah—the Devil's Horn. Infuriated at the influence Ross held over the majority of Cherokees, John Ridge wrote to Governor Wilson Lumpkin of Georgia asking for the help of the Georgia Guard. From this came the arrests of several pro-Ross leaders, including the much-respected Elijah Hicks.

Following Georgia's takeover of Cherokee homes, land, and other property, the Cherokee national council had concluded that an itemization of their losses should be made for use in any future treaties with the United States. A committee of five Cherokee men had been appointed to the task. Elijah Hicks and J. J. Trott were engaged in this work in northern Georgia when they were arrested by the Georgia Guard. They were tied with ropes and marched off to Springplace, Georgia, where they were held for some ten or more days. When a writ of habeas corpus secured them a court hearing, the two Cherokees were shuffled about from location to location through swamps and mountains to avoid legal process.

Finally the two men were each required to post a bond of a thousand dollars. When they did so and appeared in court, the case against them was dropped. The men were released, but their books and papers were never returned.

The division between the two Cherokee groups was further intensified when Stand Watie, the brother of Elias Boudinot, seized the Cherokee printing press and other paraphernalia. Rancor ran deep among both Cherokee factions. John Walker, Jr., a member of the Treaty party, had been ambushed, shot, and killed the previous September. Now there were threats being made against the Ridges and Boudinot. Having no proof of collusion at the time, the Ross men stayed their hand.

Schermerhorn presented Jackson's new treaty proposal at the Red Clay council of October 1835. He offered the terms agreed on at Boudinot's house earlier. Fearing that they would be assassinated otherwise, members of the Treaty party joined in with the Ross party in rejecting the treaty offer. But it was a false show of resistance. They had by no means given up on their intentions. Even from Red Clay, John Ridge wrote to Lumpkin, telling of plans to make a new treaty in December. He also sought reassurances that Boudinot's property would not be confiscated.

It would be unfair to say that the Cherokee men who favored the treaty were disloyal to their people or indifferent to their welfare. They had honestly come to the conclusion that it would be better to accept the inevitable loss of their homeland, where they were surrounded and overwhelmed. To them it was clear that it was best for the Cherokees to move off to the West, where they could reshape their own destiny unmolested by whites. After all, other Cherokees of intelligence and consequence—Sequoyah was cited as an example—had already made that decision and were happy with it.

The Treaty party charged that John Ross had, for his own selfish economic purposes, duped the masses of uneducated Cherokees. Most tribespeople, they argued, were too ignorant to realize that they were better off giving up their homes and moving west than fighting to hold them. In a presentation to Congress, the Treaty men argued that "it is a mistaken idea that a majority would prefer to remain here at the hazard of State subjection."

At Red Clay, Ross had secured the council's authorization to lead a delegation to Washington to negotiate a treaty. It was the evident work of a U.S.-Georgia Treaty party conspiracy when a squad of the Georgia Guard illegally crossed the Tennessee line on the night of December 5, 1835, and arrested Ross and Payne. The two men were forced to ride through a blinding rainstorm to Camp Benton at the former Springplace Mission in Georgia. There

NO TREATY AT ALL

A letter from Major William M. Davis to Lewis Cass, Secretary of War, March 5, 1836:

I conceive, sir that my duty to the President, to yourself, and to my country, reluctantly compels me to make a statement to you of facts in relation to a meeting of a small number of Cherokees at New Echota last December, who were met by Mr. Schermerhorn, as U.S. commissioner, and articles of a general treaty entered into between them for the whole Cherokee Nation.

Sir, that paper, containing the articles entered into at New Echota in December last, called a treaty, is no treaty at all, because [it was] not sanctioned by the great body of the Cherokee people, and made without their consent or participation in it, pro or con; and I here solemnly declare to you, without hesitation, that upon a reference of this treaty to the Cherokee people, it would be instantly rejected by more than nine-tenths of them; in fact, I incline to the belief that nineteen-twentieths would rise up against it.

The Indians had long been notified of the meeting, and every pains taken to induce them to come in; blankets were promised gratis to all who would come and go for a treaty. A very inflammatory address against the chiefs, and urging the Indians to attend the treaty, was written by Mr. Schermerhorn, translated, and printed in the Cherokee alphabet and language, and extensively circulated. But all to no purpose, a mere handful attended, and they were the remnants of the old Ross and Ridge parties, many of whom would not have attended the meeting at all but through fear of being legislated out of their homes by Georgia, and were induced to believe that, by attending the treaty, they could retain their homes a while longer.

The most cunning and artful means were resorted to, to conceal the paucity and smallness of the number of Indians present at the treaty; their numbers were not taken down by the commissioner. He doubtless had no wish to do so, for they were too small to answer his purpose. You could not ascertain them from the issues of provisions, as I am credibly informed they were irregular and not strictly according to numbers present. The business of making the treaty was transacted with a committee appointed by the Indians present, and not with all of them present—that would expose their numbers.

And if I am not misinformed, the power of attorney under which the committee acted, was not signed by every Indian present but by the chairman and secretary of the meeting—for that would expose their weakness. It does therefore appear to me that Mr. Schermerhorn designed to conceal the real

> number present, and to impose on the public and the Government upon this point; the greatest pains were taken by him to puff the number present and to puff the treaty.
>
> Mr. Schermerhorn, in order to carry out his scheme of deception more effectually, took on with him to Washington a large delegation, selected from among the few who attended the New Echota meeting, and who formed a considerable portion of that meeting. But, sir, that delegation had no more authority to make a treaty for the whole nation than any other dozen Cherokee accidently picked for that purpose; they are not the delegation of the Cherokee nation, nor have they power or authority to act for them.

they were held in a damp, windowless log cabin. Ross and Payne were held without being charged for thirteen days.

This was long enough for Schermerhorn, through the use of threats and bribes, to bring together at New Echota some 300 to 500 of the 17,000 Cherokee population. Neither John Ross nor any of his supporters were present when on December 29, John Ridge, Major Ridge, Elias Boudinot, Stand Watie, William Hicks, An-

Red Clay, Tennessee, Council Ground marker. *(Photo by Stan Hoig)*

drew Ross, David Vann, William S. Coodey, and fewer than 100 other Cherokees met. This minority group signed a highly questionable treaty by which the United States purchased the lands of the Cherokee Nation for $5 million. By the pact—called the Treaty of New Echota—the Cherokees agreed to their own removal west.

Ross and the Cherokee national council immediately protested the treaty, declaring that it had been made by individuals who had no authority whatever. Their protest was supported by the signatures of 14,910 Cherokees, reflecting the firestorm of anger that swept through the Cherokee rank and file. Dire threats against the Treaty party men were expressed openly.

Schermerhorn's activities in arranging the treaty had been so spurious that army officer Major William M. Davis felt compelled to write a letter of complaint to Secretary of War Lewis Cass. Davis, a Kentuckian whose father had been an officer during the Revolutionary War, had served both under Cass during the War of 1812 and with Andrew Jackson in the Battle of New Orleans. In 1831 he had been appointed to the task of enrolling Cherokees for removal. Davis charged that by making himself completely disliked by the Indians, Schermerhorn had done more to prolong the problem of removal than to resolve it.

Leaders of the Treaty group—William Rogers, Elias Boudinot, John Ridge, and Stand Watie—defended Schermerhorn against Davis's attack, insisting that the commissioner had acted with the best of motives toward the Indians and that no other individual could have done better. They pointed out that Ross himself was now willing to sell the Cherokee land and repeated the charge that he had won his following by duping an ignorant people.

Ross and his followers responded to the New Echota treaty by hurrying to Washington with a petition pleading with the Senate not to ratify the compact. The Ross delegation, however, was told contemptuously that they would not be recognized unless "you unite with the delegates appointed by the general council of the Cherokee nation in December last, after their adoption of the proffered treaty, and in pursuance of instructions from that body, sign the adopted treaty, and co-operate with the delegation chosen."

Both the Ross delegation and Major Davis's report were ignored. Their arguments were countered by Lumpkin, who wrote to Jackson that "nineteen-twentieths of the Cherokees are too ignorant and depraved to entitle their opinions to any weight or consideration in such matters." By a single vote, the U.S. Senate approved the treaty, and on May 23, 1836, President Andrew Jackson victoriously signed it into law.

John Quincy Adams, the former president and political foe of Jackson, led in a public outcry. He described the treaty as "infamous . . . it brings with it eternal disgrace upon the country."

NOTES

p. 46   "solitary tree . . " Grace Steele Woodward, *The Cherokees* (Norman: University of Oklahoma Press, 1963), p. 175.

p. 46   "If we determine . . ." Wilson Lumpkin, *The Removal of the Cherokee Indians from Georgia,* 2 vols. (New York: Dodd Mead Co., 1907), p. 52.

p. 49   "I reckon now . . ." Currey to Cass, Oct. 1, 1831, *Sen. Exec. Doc. No. 512,* 23rd Cong., 1st sess., pp. 612–15.

p. 51   "it is a mistaken idea . . ." *House Exec. Doc. No. 91,* 23rd Cong., 2d sess., p. 5.

p. 52   "I conceive, sir . . ." *HofR Doc. 286,* 24th Cong., 1st sess., pp. 148–54.

p. 54   "you unite with . . ." *House Exec. Doc. No. 286,* 24th Cong., 1st sess., pp. 432–33.

p. 55   "nineteen-twentieths . . ." Foreman, *Indian Removal,* p. 269, n. 9.

p. 55   "infamous . . ." Woodward, *The Cherokees,* p. 193.

Early Removals

On January 16, 1834, the Reverend Henry Wilson, Jr. wrote from New Dwight Mission in the Indian Territory near present Vian, Oklahoma. He told of the dire conditions suffered by the Cherokees who had migrated there: "Driven from the homes of their fathers to the very utmost verge of our country, they know not what to do or where to go. O! Could you see the wrongs which these poor people suffer."

The torment of the Cherokees in moving west had been taking place for a long time. Some went overland by wagon, some by river flatboat, and some in small independent parties. There had been a steady migration from the Old Nation to the Arkansas country since the first group under Chief Tahlonteskee arrived there in 1810. It and some of the large government-conducted contingents such as the Jolly party of 1819 used the boat route. This was down the Tennessee, Ohio, and Mississippi rivers to Montgomery's Point at the mouth of the White and Arkansas rivers. Others used a northern wagon route across Kentucky, Illinois, and Missouri, the one that would set the pattern for the final great exodus over the Trail of Tears in 1838.

A more direct land route was often followed by smaller parties of Cherokees. It led along the southern Tennessee border to Memphis, formerly known as the Chickasaw Bluffs. There the great Mississippi River could be crossed by ferry. Travelers could continue overland across the Chickasaw country to the Arkansas River in a much shorter time.

This route was followed by those driving stock for emigrating groups. Additionally, there was an occasional interchange of visitors who used this connection between the Eastern and the Western Cherokees—Old Nation residents making sojourns to the West; Western residents returning to the Old Nation, either temporarily or permanently.

The records are by no means complete regarding all of the migrations that occurred. However, it was clearly a continuing affair. An item in the *Missionary Herald* of June 1823 noted that forty to fifty Cherokee families from the lower towns had passed by Dwight Mission in Arkansas on their way to settle upstream. They were in a miserable condition and begged for supplies.

The *Arkansas Gazette* of Little Rock occasionally mentioned Cherokee immigrants arriving. In March 1829, it reported that forty to fifty families were in boats at the mouth of the White River. In April, the newspaper announced that the steamboat *James O'Hara* had arrived from Louisville with sixty-five more Cherokees, who looked more white than Indian. In May, it said that the *O'Hara* was back with some 100 more of the same. The June 24 issue of the paper told of the steamer *Facility* arriving with a keelboat in tow containing several Cherokee families. During February 1830, the paper observed that the riverboat *Industry* had reached Little Rock with some 200 Cherokees and their slaves; in March it said that seventy to eighty more emigrants had passed by.

In March 1832, the newspaper mentioned more Cherokees who were at the mouth of the White, with 500 others on the way from the Old Nation. It also reported that a Cherokee woman named Vann, about sixty years of age, had fallen overboard from her keelboat at night and was lost. In May, the *Arkansas Gazette* announced that the *Thomas Yeatman* had passed by with 400 more Cherokees from Alabama and returned after landing them at Fort Gibson.

In April 1832, emigration agent Ben Currey set out by boat for Arkansas from Hiwassee Garrison opposite the mouth of the Hiwassee River with some 626 Cherokees. In these removals, the government failed to provide the food and supplies it had promised. As a result, the emigrants suffered severely, enduring much illness and death. They sent word back to others strongly advising them not to leave their homes.

Cherokee Alexander Thompson, who had migrated to the Indian Territory in the spring of 1830, returned to the Old Nation after a year and a half. He warned other Cherokees that he had been poorly received and had suffered from rampant sickness. His neighbors, he declared, were lazy and corrupted by stealing and other bad habits. In his estimate, the soil and climate were unfavorable. Good water was scarce, he said, and game could be found only at a great distance.

Even as Reverend Wilson was writing his letter in 1834, a group of Cherokee emigrants had been gathered in log pens at the Hiwassee Garrison. There they were besieged by whiskey dealers who plied the Tennessee River in boats. Lieutenant Joseph W. Harris, a West Pointer who was conductor for the group, diligently recorded events of the removal in his diary. In order to get the money that had been issued to the Indians for removal, white vendors promoted drunken parties that made the tribesmen easy prey and often resulted in bloody quarrels.

After much delay, on March 13 two flatboats holding seventy-two of the emigrants were carried off southward in the current of the Tennessee River. A few days later, the remainder of the Indians were boarded onto four more flatboats. After six days of dodging snags and uprooted trees in the river, negotiating the famous "Suck" whirlpool near Lookout Mountain, and passing through the treacherous Muscle Shoals, the two groups consolidated at Waterloo, Alabama.

Having picked up some Cherokees at Creek Path, the party now consisted of 457 emigrants. These were loaded aboard the river steamer *Thomas Yeatman* and three keelboats that it towed. The remainder of the voyage saw frequent stops to refuel at wood yards along the rivers to repair the steamboat's machinery or paddle wheel or to pause and bury a member who had died.

In one instance, a Cherokee woman who had been cooking aboard a keelboat at night slipped and fell into the swift current. There was no chance to save her; with one wild shriek she was gone into the dark waters. It was not a particularly unusual occurrence on the water migration route. On another occasion, a party of sixty-seven Cherokees was met on the river. Their boat was filling with water, and the occupants, few of whom could swim, faced certain drowning. Lieutenant Harris responded to their pleas and crammed them aboard his vessels. Their boat sank soon after.

At Montgomery's Point, the party found another 200 Cherokees who had been transporting themselves in a fleet of eight or nine flatboats. Harris gave in to the pleas of his passengers to take them on even though they had suffered much from the measles and had had several deaths. Thus far the trip had been downstream. Now in going up the Arkansas against its current, stymied by shoals and swifts, the traveling was much slower. Harris and his charges arrived at Little Rock on April 9, but at the mouth of Cadron Creek the water became too shallow for the paddle wheeler. Harris had no choice but to put ashore and make a camp where the numerous sick could be cared for.

The situation was made even more alarming when on April 15 the camp was swept by cholera. The panic-stricken Indians scattered through the woods, building their fires well apart from one another. Though untrained medically, Harris did all he could to care for his charges.

The Cherokees continued to die; there was little that could be done for them. Dr. Roberts, the country doctor attending them, could offer only doses of opium and calomel. Yet under his treatment, the deaths began to slacken off. But then he, too, died.

"I have devoted the day to my poor friend," Harris wrote in his diary on that day. "He has none to help him! His poor weakly wife can scarcely crawl about; the only servant is better out of the way,

DEATH AT CADRON CREEK

From the journal of Lieutenant Joseph Harris, on board the *Thomas Yeatman,* Cadron Creek, Arkansas Territory, April 16, 1834:

The sun rose bright & clear in the heavens this morning and shed around the brilliant beams of an April day. To us it should have been a day of Clouds. Such gorgeous glories mock the wickedness they shone upon. Notes of lamentation & of woe rose upon the morning air & the shrieks of the dying! Insatiate death stalks through our little camp & with a conspiring & awfully disfiguring hand, greedily gathers his victims to the garner. Every hope of yesterday has vanished—that all sweeping scourge the malignant cholera is in our tents, & has scattered dismay & horror around us. There were more cases of death before breakfast, and eleven in all before the sun went down. At 10 a.m. I dispatched an express to Little Rock for further medical assistance, requesting by letters the aid and advice of Drs. Sprague & See, & the personal attendance of them. A number of my people are now down with sickness of various kinds; and all are panic struck and scattering through the woods building their campfires as remote from each other as their several fears direct them, and all are, I am afraid, but too well prepared to receive this terrible disease, if they have not the seeds of it within them already.

It is impossible for one physician to administer to them all. I have held a consultation with Dr. Roberts & have turned nurse & doctor myself and my blood chills even as I write, at the remembrance of the scenes I have gone through today. In the cluster of cedars upon the bluff which looks down upon the Creek & river, and near a few tall chimneys—the wreck of a once comfortable tenement, the destroyer has been most busily at work. Three large families of the poor class are there encamped, & I have passed much of the day with them, & have devoted the larger portion of my cares to these sufferers—but in vain were my efforts; the hand of death was upon them. At one time I saw stretched around me and within a few feet of each other, eight of these afflicted creatures dead or dying. Yet no loud lamentations went up from the bereaved ones here. They were of the true Indian blood. They looked upon the departed ones with a manly sorrow & silently mourned over the end we all must come to. Quietly they digged graves for their dead, and as quietly they laid them out in their narrow beds. They saw in it a fearful visitation of the Great Spirit & knew not how soon their own hour might be at hand. There was a dignity in their grief which is sublime; and which, poor and destitute, ignorant and unbefriended as they were, made me respect them.

or has her hands full to keep this houseful of children from their dying father."

The country was undergoing a severe drought, with no hope that the river would soon rise. Going back to Little Rock, Harris finally managed to hire ox teams and wagons for taking the Indians on by land. By the time the wagons arrived, he himself had taken sick. Knowing that the drivers might well desert if he did not proceed immediately, Harris struggled out of his blankets and climbed aboard his horse. The wagons were loaded with the sick, and all who could walk were required to carry their own provisions. Most of the Indians had to leave behind their most prized possessions. Death still stalked the pathetic entourage as it headed up the banks of the Arkansas.

Harris made long rides ahead of the Indians to search for food. However, a great flood of the Arkansas River the prior June had wiped out crops along the Arkansas valley, and the country was in destitute condition. Occasionally he would find a small supply of corn or pork. Finally, on May 10, Harris and his party made camp on Sallisaw Creek near New Dwight Mission in the Indian Territory. From there in the days following, the Cherokees began dispersing throughout the Western Cherokee country.

Harris arrived at Fort Gibson on May 14 and made his reports. During the trip west, there had been eighty-one deaths among the Cherokee emigrants. Fifty were from cholera. Forty-five of the dead had been children, who died chiefly of measles, dysentery, worms, and exposure. Many more would die during the plague of sickness that swept through the Indian Territory that year. Totally exhausted, Harris returned East. He continued in the Indian service until 1837 when, his health ruined, he died at his home in Portsmouth, New Hampshire, his heroic efforts on behalf of the Cherokees little known.

Following ratification of the Treaty of New Echota in 1835, the U.S. government had stepped up its efforts to enlist Cherokees and escort them west. The first to migrate under the false treaty were 600 or more pro-treaty people who gathered at New Echota in January 1837. They represented the wealthy elite of the Cherokee Nation. Some of them—in sharp contrast to the Ross people—had received handsome compensation for their relinquished land, property, and stock. The fine carriages in which the warmly dressed families rode, the stout wagons loaded with personal goods, the finely groomed saddle horses, the fatted oxen, and the numerous black servants were in great contrast to the desperately poor, captive emigrants who would follow. As planned, this group arrived at their new homesites in time to plant spring crops.

In early March of 1837, a group of 466 Cherokees, half of whom were children, had been gathered in a camp at Ross's Landing (now a part of Chattanooga). This was a voluntary migration, but many of the Cherokees had been virtually shanghaied or tricked into leaving their homes. Most had been lured into migrating by the expense money paid them in advance by the government—money they often threw away in gambling and drunken revelry while waiting to leave. Finally, on March 3, eleven flatboats loaded with emigrants, their possessions, and foodstuff—cornmeal, flour, and bacon—set forth down the Tennessee River.

This migration included several significant figures. Most notable were Major Ridge, a leader of the Treaty party; Boudinot's brother, Stand Watie, destined to become a Confederate general during the Civil War; Watie's uncle, Charles Reese, who had led the capture of Creek canoes during the Battle of Horseshoe Bend; Elijah Hicks, only recently released from a Georgia prison but soon to be an important Western Cherokee judge; and Turtle Fields, a licensed Methodist preacher and close friend of Sequoyah.

A cold, damp wind whipped about the unprotected boat occupants. There had been much whiskey drinking by the Indians before departure, and it would continue through the trip. There seemed always to be white men with whiskey for sale, either at the town ports or from whiskey boats that plied the river. The problem plagued the party commander, General Nathaniel Smith, as well as Dr. C. Lillybridge, who chronicled the journey.

Major Ridge, who assassinated Doublehead over Cherokee land, was himself assassinated for his part in the Treaty of New Echota. *(Archives & Manuscripts,
Oklahoma Historical Society)*

The emigrants floated downstream on the flatboats to Gunter's
Landing (now Guntersville), Alabama. From there they were
hitched to the steamboat *Knoxville* and towed to the head of
Muscle Shoals. In order to detour around the dangerous shoals,
the Indians were loaded onto railroad flatcars. This was a unique,

though wet and cold, experience. At Tuscumbia, Alabama they were transferred to two keelboats that were overcrowded, without stoves, and had water in their holds.

Under tow by the steamer *Newark,* the emigrant party floated on to the junction of the Tennessee and Ohio rivers at Paducah, Kentucky. Then it was on down the Ohio and the Mississippi past Memphis to Montgomery's Point. Picking up a river pilot there, the entourage of boats made its way up the Arkansas River past sandbars and snags to Little Rock, Van Buren, Fort Smith, and finally their boat destination at Fort Coffee, Indian Territory. They arrived at Coffee on March 28. The journey had been agonizingly long and fraught with delays. Exposure to cold, rain, and snow in the open boats contributed to numerous colds, pleurisy, dysentery, fever, and diarrhea. But though they suffered considerably, this group had been very fortunate in making the trip without losing a single member.

The emigrating party that departed by wagon over the land route on October 14, 1837 was not as blessed. Under the charge of Lieutenant B. B. Cannon, the emigrant wagon train set out from the Cherokee agency at Calhoun, Tennessee. Three days later, they crossed the Tennessee by ferry and spent the next four days struggling over the Cumberland Plateau to reach McMinnville. They buried their first child near Murfreesboro on the twenty-fifth.

From there to Nashville, the group passed through three turnpike gates and crossed over the Cumberland River on a toll bridge. Another child was buried near Hopkinsville, Kentucky on November 8, and still another on the thirteenth after crossing the Mississippi River near Jonesboro, Illinois. Many now became sick from drinking stagnant water and eating wild grapes. The weather became intensely cold soon after the caravan passed Caledonia, Missouri on November 23. When sixty of the members became too ill to travel, a halt was called for some ten days. Three Cherokee children and a black youngster who served as a wagoner died there.

It began snowing, and temperatures fell even lower as Cannon's party struggled across southern Missouri, passing through Springfield and there turning south to Cane Hill, Arkansas. The officer's diary now became a listing of deaths on the trail.

> December 8th—Buried Nancy Bigbears Grand Child. December 15th–December 17—Buried Elleges wife and Charles Timberlakes son (Smoker). December 18th— Buried Dreadful Waters this evening. The ancient chief had signed the Treaty of 1817. December 22nd—Buried Goddards Grand Child. December 23rd—Buried Rainfrogs daughter (Lucy Redstick's child). December 27th—Buried Alsey Timberlake, daughter of Chas. Timberlake. December 28th—Buried another child of Chas. Timberlakes, and one which was born (untimely).

At least two other children were born during the journey. In all there had been at least fifteen deaths on the march, eleven of them children. Upon reaching a point just inside the Indian Territory, the group was turned over to an officer from Fort Gibson, who escorted them on to his post.

A smaller independent wagon party was on the road westward at the same time as the Cannon-led group. The John Ridge and Elias Boudinot families, along with the William Lassley family and a woman named Polly Gilbreath, had departed Creek Path, Alabama during mid-October of 1837 headed for the Indian Territory. They, too, took the northern route through Nashville, where Ridge paid a courtesy visit to ex-president Andrew Jackson at his Hermitage home.

It is uncertain what route they took from there. Cherokee historian Thurman Wilkins thought that they might have followed the same route as the Cannon party across southern Missouri. The Ridge-Boudinot entourage, however, arrived at the new home site on Honey Creek, Indian Territory in late November, a month sooner than the Cannon party.

Apparently, they endured little of the trauma suffered by the Cannon party, who were on the trail just behind them. Perhaps Ridge and Boudinot had simply got ahead of the bad weather and

JOHN RIDGE,

A CHEROKEE.

John Ridge knew that as a leader of the Treaty party he risked being killed, as he was shortly after the Cherokee removal. *(Archives & Manuscripts, Oklahoma Historical Society)*

moved much faster because of their small numbers. Or it could be that they took a more direct route across western Tennessee and northern Arkansas.

These final migrations of 1837 had set the stage. The misery and deaths endured by the Cannon group were no more than harbingers of the final great removals of 1838, most of which were by way of the northern land route.

NOTES

p. 56   "Driven from the homes . . ." *Cherokee Phoenix*, May 24, 1834.

p. 59   "I have devoted . . ." Journal of Lieut. Joseph Harris, Cherokee Removal, Section X, Archives/Manuscripts, Oklahoma Historical Society.

p. 60   "The sun rose . . ." Journal of Lieut. Joseph Harris.

p. 65   "December 8th . . ." Lieutenant B. B. Cannon Diary, Special File 249, C553, RG 75, National Archives.

The Politics of Survival

In the fall of 1837, English geologist George W. Featherstonhaugh made a journey through the Cherokee country in Tennessee and Georgia. During a visit to Red Clay, he had the opportunity to attend a Cherokee Sunday morning worship. Present were not only many Cherokees who dressed much like whites but also traditional tribesmen with their red and blue turbans, embroidered hunting shirts, and deerskin leggings. The Englishman was greatly impressed.

> This spectacle insensibly led me into reflection upon the opinion which is so generally entertained of its being impossible to civilize the Indians in our sense of the word. Here is a remarkable instance which seems to furnish a conclusive answer to skepticism on this point. A whole Indian nation abandons the pagan practices of their ancestors, adopts the Christian religion, uses books printed in their own language, submits to the government of their elders, builds houses and temples of worship, relies upon agriculture for their support, and produces men of great ability to rule over them, and to whom they give a willing obedience. Are not these the great principles of civilization? They are driven from their religious and social state then, not because they cannot be civilized, but

> because a pseudo set of civilized beings, who are too
> strong for them, want their possessions!

By the Treaty of New Echota, removal of the Cherokees was to be effected within two years, the deadline being set at May 23, 1838. The U.S. government now ceased to recognize the existence of the Cherokee Nation government, and it was determined that any further efforts by John Ross would be suppressed.

But Ross had not given up. With bulldog resolve, he plunged ahead with his efforts to save the Cherokee Nation from removal. In late 1836 Ross made a trip to visit the Western Cherokees, seeking their support in opposing the treaty. The Western Cherokees responded to Ross's plea with a petition to Congress asking that the Treaty of New Echota be rescinded.

They requested this on the grounds that the treaty was "calculated to effect injuriously the interests and happiness of both parts of the Cherokee family." The lead signature was that of George Guess (Sequoyah), who lent his famous name to Ross's cause.

Currey and other federal authorities exerted as much pressure on the Cherokee people as possible. They were generous in supplying those who signed up for removal with food and other goods. The many who did not sign up, however, were cut off from their own treaty-promised rewards and left to forage for subsistence as best they could.

In a plea to Congress in June 1836, Ross and his supporters decried the "barbarity practiced towards the Cherokees" by Currey. They claimed that he had openly declared it government policy to make the situation of the Indians so miserable as to force them into a treaty. They cited many instances of Currey's callousness.

A Cherokee woman was persuaded to enroll for emigration, but her husband refused. Agents returned later and took her and their children by force and sent them off to Arkansas, leaving the husband behind. A Cherokee man was enrolled while drunk, but when the time came to depart, he could not be found. Currey sent troops to arrest the man's wife and children. They were held under guard all night, cold and shivering, until the woman agreed to

TAKEOVER AT VANN'S HOUSE

Today the Vann house at Chatsworth, Georgia has been handsomely restored. Built in 1805 by Cherokee town chief James Vann, it no longer bears the marks of the gun battle that once occurred there when Georgians fought over the house and its property as spoils in the Cherokee removal.

James's son Joseph, who had swum the river and fought at Horseshoe Bend, inherited the home. His considerable wealth included the slave-operated plantation and a toll ferry

Joseph Vann house near Chatsworth, Georgia.   *(Photo by Stan Hoig)*

on the federal turnpike running from Augusta, Georgia to Tennessee. In addition to the fine home, he owned mills, kitchen, slave quarters, orchards, and some 800 acres of land under cultivation.

Vann's estate became a lucrative prize when Georgia set up a lottery system by which to assign the homes of Cherokees to whites. The state declared that he had broken a state law in hiring a white man as an overseer and, as a result, had forfeited his right of occupancy. In early 1834 a citizen named Riley came to the house armed for battle and took it over. When a state agent arrived with a posse to dislodge Riley in favor of the agent's brother, a fierce gun battle ensued.

Vann and his family hid in a room and trembled in fear as bullets whizzed back and forth. Unable to dislodge Riley, the posse set fire to the house. Finally Riley surrendered, and the fire was put out.

But Vann and his family were forced out of their home in the cold and snow of winter. They fled to Tennessee, where they took shelter in an open, dirt-floored cabin.

They lived in the cabin until removing to the Indian Territory. There Vann constructed a replica of the Georgia house at Webbers Falls only to have it burned to the ground during the Civil War.

place her name on the emigration roll. When the husband came in, they were all put aboard a boat and taken to Arkansas. When two of their three children died there, the Cherokee couple returned to the Old Nation on foot.

Sconatachee, an old Cherokee man, had also enrolled while drunk but refused to come in to the emigration collection point. Currey and his interpreter went after him, but the old man held them off with a pistol. Later, Currey sent a squad after him. He was arrested and bound, then hauled off and deported. His children were left behind in the woods where they had hidden.

Cherokee Richard Cheek had enrolled before he went to work on a government railroad near Tuscumbia, Alabama. When he did not appear to emigrate, his wife was captured and shipped off to

Arkansas. She was refused permission to see her husband as her boat passed by Tuscumbia. She died during the trip.

Ross continued to speak out strongly against enforcement of the New Echota treaty. He said that his people would never recognize it as being legitimate. Playing for time, he worked to get a new treaty made, one by which the Cherokees could retain some of their Old Nation land. He lobbied in Congress and presented a

GENERAL JOHN E. WOOL.

General John E. Wool resigned his command rather than carry out removal of the Cherokees. (Gleason's Pictorial Drawing Room Companion, *June 28, 1857*)

Cherokee petition with 15,665 Cherokee signatures refuting the treaty. He had hoped to find a friend in the Van Buren administration that took office in 1837. Georgians, however, had convinced the president that the Cherokees were on the point of armed resistance, and Van Buren stiffened in his resolve to enforce the removal.

Soon after the treaty had been ratified and signed into law, the War Department ordered General John Ellis Wool to begin the process of disarming the Cherokees and preparing them for removal. But Wool was too much of a man of conscience for the chore. Calling a meeting of the Cherokees, he attempted to persuade them to cooperate with the government. Instead, he himself was persuaded to their view. On February 18, 1837, he reported to his superiors that he found the Cherokees almost universally opposed to the treaty. They were so determined to oppose the treaty, he insisted, that they would not accept either rations or clothing from the United States. This, despite the fact that they were so poor and destitute that they had been living on roots and the sap of trees. Many said that they would die before leaving their country.

Wool proceeded with the disarming of the Cherokees. At the same time, he tried to protect them from the scores of whites who flooded their country with whiskey for the purpose of robbing them. The situation was particularly bad in Alabama, where many Cherokees were dispossessed by whites. The state attempted to have Wool restrained from interfering in the Cherokees' behalf and demanded that he be investigated. Charges were brought against him in a military court at Knoxville. Alabama offered no evidence against Wool, and he was acquitted.

But Wool had had enough of his onerous task. He tendered his resignation, declaring:

> If I could, and I could not do them a greater kindness, I
> would remove every Indian tomorrow beyond the reach
> of the white men, who, like vultures, are watching,
> ready to pounce upon their prey and strip them of every-

thing they have or expect from the government of the
United States.

Brigadier General R. G. Dunlap, who commanded Tennessee
volunteer forces, had similar difficulty in carrying out his assign-
ment to undertake removal preparations. He had put his men to
work building stockades at the Cherokee agency near Calhoun,
Tennessee. The sixteen-foot-square picket enclosures were to be
used for holding the Cherokees prior to their removal. At night
the Tennessee troops attended dances and parties and became
enamored of the dark-eyed Cherokee girls, many of whom had
attended mission schools or seminaries. Both the troops and Dunlap began to find it repulsive to round up and imprison the
Cherokee people by force. Dunlap threatened to resign rather than
dishonor the military arms of Tennessee.

In August 1837, 2,000 Cherokees again assembled at Red Clay.
They had come to hear the report of Chief Ross and his delegation
on their recent visit to Washington. They were anxious to know if
any progress had been made in rescinding the Treaty of New
Echota. The Cherokee multitude huddled outside in the pouring
rain as U.S. special agent John Mason, Jr., protected by the cover
of the open-sided council house, addressed them.

He first assured them that the newly elected president, Martin
Van Buren, was the true friend of the Cherokees and that he loved
them with the same regard he felt for their white brethren. Because
of this great love, Mason said, the president wished to save them
from the evils resulting from contact with the white population
by removing them to the West. Mason neglected to say that the
government had already relocated a group of Creeks on precisely
the same land—land that was additionally occupied by the Western Cherokees under the Treaty of 1828.

Mason lashed out at Ross and his followers, telling the
drenched Cherokees not to listen to those who opposed the be-
nevolence of the government. "They are wicked men," he declared; "they speak with a forked tongue, and their bad advice
would lead to your inevitable ruin." When the agent had ended,

the crowd gave a scornful collective murmur of disgust and dispersed.

Writing from the council grounds on August 17, missionary Evan Jones expressed the Cherokees' hope that "friends of justice and humanity will unite . . . to avert the destruction which the late fraudulent arrangements threaten to the defenseless and unoffending Cherokees."

Ross responded to Mason with a letter stating that the Cherokees were very troubled to learn that Andrew Jackson's successor held the New Echota "pretended compact" to be valid. The unyielding Cherokee leader was soon in Washington, D.C. with still another delegation. He remained there during the winter of 1837–38, lobbying Congress and trying to arrange a compromise treaty that the government would accept. He also worked to collect back payments owed the Cherokees by the government and won the release of Samuel Worcester and Elizur Butler under their promise to leave Georgia.

The Ross-led Cherokee cause was not without its outspoken white supporters. Among them was Jeremiah Evarts, who wrote a series of twelve essays defending the rights and welfare of Indians. These appeared in the *Daily National Intelligencer* of Washington, D.C. under the pseudonym of William Penn. Further, the *Cherokee Phoenix* was circulated to other newspapers, which repeated its editorials.

In addition there were expressions of public conscience on behalf of the Cherokees. When the U.S. Senate rejected a petition from the Ross delegation to delay the removal, a group of 200 Marietta, Ohio citizens sent a declaration on behalf of the Cherokees. In Philadelphia, outraged citizens filled Pennsylvania Hall to adopt a resolution that condemned the government's action and declared:

> At this time when the liberties of a noble but unfortunate race are about to be closed down by the cupidity of an avaricious people; when a stain is about to be cast upon our National Escutcheon which the tears and regrets of after ages will never be able to remove, it becomes the

Renowned as an Indian fighter, General Winfield Scott organized a large military force that rounded up the Cherokees and herded them into stockade camps. (Gleason's Pictorial Drawing Room Companion, *July 19, 1851*)

duty of all the friends of humanity to raise their voices against the measures and the men who would thus entail disgrace upon this country and ruin upon its aboriginal inhabitants.

While in Washington, Ross met with General Winfield Scott, who had been assigned as Wool's replacement in removing Cherokees. In the meeting, the diminutive Cherokee leader won the respect and admiration of the towering, bulky officer, establishing a rapport that would serve Ross and the Cherokees well during the difficult months ahead.

Removal agent Ben Currey died and was replaced by General Nathaniel Smith of Tennessee. Smith proceeded to arrange for the removal of those Cherokees who were willing, or could be persuaded, to migrate. He ordered the construction of a fleet of large keelboats. These featured a 20' x 100' deckhouse partitioned into rooms and cooking hearths on the top deck.

The removal effort that had been under way for many years would now be intensified. During 1837 and the spring of 1838, six major migration groups of Cherokees would be escorted to the Indian Territory under military supervision. Though some of these were said to be voluntary removals, a great deal of government intimidation and false persuasion were employed. Altogether, fewer than 4,000 Indians were involved. A majority of the Cherokee Nation, an estimated 15,000 people, remained in the stockade camps.

NOTES

p. 68   "This spectacle . . ." George W. Featherstonhaugh, *A Canoe Voyage up the Minnay Sotor* (London: R. Bentley, 1847), pp. 229–33.

p. 69   "calculated to effect . . ." Resolution of Western Cherokees, *House Exec. Doc. No. 99,* 25th Cong., 1st sess., pp. 14–15.

p. 69   "barbarity practiced . . ." *House Exec. Doc. No. 286,* p. 8.

p. 73   "If I could . . ." Grant Foreman, *Indian Removal,* pp. 271–72.

p. 74   "They are wicked men . . ." Address of John Mason, Jr., *House Exec. Doc. No. 99,* 25th Cong., 1st sess., p. 34.

p. 75   "friends of justice . . ." *Baptist Missionary Magazine,* April 1838, p. 94.

p. 75   "At this time . . ." Woodward, *The Cherokees,* pp. 200–201.

Search and Seizure

Fifty-two-year-old General Winfield Scott, nicknamed "Old Fuss and Feathers," had negotiated treaties with northern tribes following the Black Hawk War. More recently he had seen action against the Seminoles in Florida. At his disposal now were the federal troops already in the Cherokee country plus militia and volunteers that could be called forth from various states. His force was to consist of 1,480 volunteer troops each from the states of Tennessee, Georgia, and Alabama and 740 from North Carolina. This plus 2,200 United States regulars would give him a total command of 7,380 men.

Three military districts were established. The Eastern district included North Carolina, part of Tennessee north of Gilmer County in Georgia, and the counties of Gilmer, Union, and Lumpkin in Georgia. Its headquarters were at Fort Butler. The Western district covered Alabama, western Tennessee, and Dade County, Georgia, with headquarters at Ross's Landing. The Middle district was composed of all the Cherokee country not in other districts and headquartered at New Echota.

Troops were put to work building stockades to be used as collection camps. There were thirty-one such forts established. Thirteen were in Georgia, eight in Tennessee, and five each in

Ross home restoration, Rossville, Tennessee. *(Photo by Stan Hoig)*

Alabama and North Carolina. From these locations, the Indians would be taken to eleven internment camps in Tennessee and Alabama. The captives would then be sent on to the main points of embarkation at the Cherokee agency at Calhoun, at Ross's Landing, or at Gunter's Landing on the Tennessee River in northern Alabama.

On May 10, 1838, Scott issued a proclamation to the Cherokee people. In it he declared that the Cherokees had delayed for two years in removing themselves and joining their people on the other side of the Mississippi. Now he had come with a powerful army to force them to do so. The troops, Scott insisted, were their friends, kindhearted and brave, and would execute their painful duty with mercy. He warned the headmen and warriors not to offer armed resistance or try to hide in the mountains and forests. He directed the Cherokees to prepare for emigration and come forward so they could be transported to their new homes.

To his troops, Scott issued a statement warning them that the majority of the Cherokees were opposed to removal. Because of this it would be necessary to take them prisoner and transport them to the removal sites. Acts of harshness and cruelty, he declared, would lead to a general war and carnage. He admonished his men to exercise every possible kindness to the Cherokees and threatened severe penalty if a soldier was found guilty of wanton injury or insult to any Cherokee man, woman, or child.

On May 17, 1838, Scott spelled out the rules of engagement for his troops. Every captured man was to be disarmed if necessary, the arms to be restored beyond the Mississippi. All strong men, women, boys, and girls would be required to march to their points of confinement under military escort. Slaves would be treated in the same manner as the Indians. Indian horses and ponies would be used to transport the feeble, along with light cooking utensils and bedding. Wagons would be supplied if needed. The Indians would be allowed to take along light articles. All other personal property—including corn, oats, fodder, and beef cattle—would be taken possession of and the owners given certificates redeemable at the depots.

Ross's Landing marker. (*Archives & Manuscripts, Oklahoma Historical Society*)

In another order, he further instructed his field commanders to surround and bring in the Indians in small groups until enough were gathered to march them to one of the three emigrating depots. Georgia governor George R. Gilmer issued a statement warning the public that the troops could not be properly organized until May 25. That was the date, he said, on which state laws ceased to recognize the Indians' right of occupancy to their homes and land. He cautioned Georgia citizens to wait until the Indians had been removed from the country and not to use force to obtain possession of their land. Otherwise, he feared, there could be a Cherokee uprising.

By Scott's order, forcible military collection of the Cherokees began on May 26. On that day, nine companies of mounted U.S. troops crossed the Coosawattie River twelve miles below New Echota. Small detachments were sent out to prevent escape. The main body of troops advanced on Indian farms and settlements along the river. The command returned to New Echota with 209 men, women, and children. There had been no bodily resistance, the officer noted, even though the Cherokees clearly were very much opposed to removal.

From Fort Hetzel in Tennessee the commanding officer reported on May 26: "I have made prisoner of 425 or perhaps 450. I think by the time I get in the outstanding members of the families that I have broken up I will have as many as I can manage. . . . They run in every instance where they have the best opportunity . . ."

Similar search and capture forays were conducted throughout the Cherokee country. Though Scott's orders had prohibited harm or cruelty in rounding up the Cherokees, the private notes of the missionaries show that these orders were seldom adhered to. Baptist missionary Evan Jones noted that the Cherokees' furniture, crops, livestock, and implements were all at the mercy of plunderers. Supposedly, government collectors would gather up the Indians' property and care for it. White neighbors, Jones observed, were seeing to it that the collectors had little to collect.

Jones's observations were echoed in the day-to-day journal of American Board missionary Daniel S. Butrick. Butrick described one instance in which two small children were frightened by the arrival of troops and fled into the woods. The captive mother pleaded in vain for permission to look for them. She was taken on to a stockade and only a couple of days later finally secured permission for a friend to go back for the children. Another woman who returned home to get her bedding found that everything in her house had been stripped away by whites.

Many families were torn apart. Men and children who were absent from their homes were seized and were not allowed to return to their families. The captives were forced to leave behind cattle, horses, hogs, household furniture, clothing—virtually everything they owned. White inhabitants, Butrick noted, stood by ready to seize whatever property they could. On June 16, 1838, Jones wrote in his own journal:

> The Cherokees are nearly all prisoners. They have been dragged from their houses, and encamped at the forts and military posts, all over the [Cherokee] nation. In Georgia, especially, multitudes were allowed no time to take any thing with them except the clothes they had on. Well-furnished houses were left a prey to plunderers, who, like hungry wolves, follow in the train of the captors. These wretches rifle the houses and strip the helpless, unoffending owners of all they have on earth. Females who have been habituated to comforts and comparative affluence are driven on foot before the bayonets of brutal men. Their feelings are mortified by the blasphemous vociferations of these heartless creatures. It is a painful sight.

By early June, the paymaster at Fort Cass, which had been established near the Calhoun, Tennessee agency, reported that 4,200 Cherokees had been gathered there. By the end of that month, Scott announced that three-fourths of the Cherokees had been collected, with 3,000 having already been sent off. In July the *Georgia Pioneer* observed that a company of Georgia mounted volunteers had recently passed by with twenty-five Indians, including a noted chief named Soft Shell Turtle. This was the last remnant of Cherokees in the country, it was believed. By late June, Georgians had begun celebrating their victory:

> Georgia troops are about to be honorably discharged from the service, having performed the duty for which they were organized—giving possession of the country to our citizens. We have only space to renew our hearty congratulations to the citizens of the State, that our Indian troubles are at last closed, we may hope, forever.

Accolades for General Scott were sounded, too. The *New York American* declared: "No laurel which Scott has acquired, will live so long as that which he has gathered in the bloodless fields of the Cherokee country." Indeed, the Cherokee capturing process had been done quietly without much public attention being drawn to it. In large part, the commercial press was determinedly silent about the ordeal. The missionary publications were virtually the only voices to cry out for the Cherokees.

One newspaper of the day observed that, had they chosen to resist, the Cherokees could have brought 4,000 warriors into the field. Though the Indians would have been exterminated eventually, the writer felt, they could have created widespread desolation throughout their country.

In August the *Hamilton Gazette*, which was printed at Ross's Landing, reported that all the Indians had been collected. Two thousand were at Ross's Landing, 8,000 at the Cherokee agency, and 800 at Fort Payne, Alabama. It further listed three removal parties that had departed from Ross's Landing during June 1838.

The first to depart was a party of 800 that left on June 6 under the command of Lieutenant Edward Deas. The Cherokees were loaded aboard six flatboats, which were lashed three to a side of a steamboat. At one point in passing through the rapids above Lookout Mountain, a barge was thrown ashore violently by the swift current, but no one was injured. At Decatur, Alabama, the Indians and their baggage were transferred to railroad cars and taken in two groups to Tuscumbia. There they were put aboard the steamboat *Smelter*, which took them the remainder of the way

THE CAPTURE OF EPENETUS ACHAIA

Epenetus Achaia and his wife were very proud of their son Jonas, who was attending the white man's mission school at Brainerd, Tennessee. But the two full-blood Cherokees missed him very much. They decided that they and their other children would attend a sacramental meeting at the school on May 3, 1838 and visit Jonas. It was more than a hundred miles through the mountains from their home in northern Georgia to Brainerd. Epenetus and the children walked while his wife rode their one horse.

After a week's visit, the Achaia family began their journey home. En route, however, they were met by a company of soldiers, who arrested them and said they were to be sent west. They were not even permitted to go home and gather their belongings. Instead the family was driven to a compound near the courthouse in Lafayette, Georgia, where some 500 other Cherokees were being held under guard.

The Cherokee captives called a meeting. They all agreed that they would have nothing to do with the money being promised them under the Treaty of New Echota. They chose Achaia to be their speaker and make their views known to the U.S. commissioner. When the time came, he told the official that the treaty had not been made by the authorities of the Cherokee Nation. He and others would have nothing to do with it. The Indians also demanded more food and medical attention for the children in the camp who were ill.

But nothing he said had any effect. Under no circumstances—not even when parents were separated from children—were any of the Cherokees permitted to return home. Achaia later learned that all of his household goods, his cows, yoke of oxen, and the goods in the little store he operated were plundered by white people.

After ten days in the Lafayette stockade, the Cherokees were marched off north to Ross's Landing on the Tennessee River. There Achaia contacted the Reverend Daniel Butrick and begged him to see about his son at Brainerd. The missionary, who was tending the sick in the camp and conducting funerals for the dead, agreed to do so.

Epenetus and his family were jammed aboard a crowded flatboat towed by a steamboat and shipped off to the Far West. Later that fall, Butrick and his wife traveled with the Cherokee mass exodus over the Trail of Tears. They brought Jonas with them and eventually united him with his family in the Indian Territory.

to the Indian Territory. They suffered no deaths; but they were in destitute condition when they were unloaded just west of Fort Smith at Fort Coffee. They did not even have tents for shelter.

The second group of 875 left Ross's Landing on June 13 in flatboats that were bound together in pairs to navigate the rapids. Downriver the boats were tied to the steamer *George Guess*. Like the previous party, they skirted Muscle Shoals by train and then reembarked on the *Smelter* with one flatboat in tow. When they reached Little Rock in early July, the low channel of the Arkansas

Lookout Mountain at the Chattanooga bend of the Tennessee River—Rossville or Ross's Landing—was a point of departure for many Cherokees traveling by boat and for the Taylor detachment that traveled the overland Trail of Tears. (Frank Leslie's Illustrated Newspaper, *January 8, 1887, courtesy Library of Congress*)

River forced them to transfer to the *Tecumseh*, which had a lighter draft. Still the boat became grounded, requiring that the emigrants be transferred to wagons. The extremely hot weather, scarcity of water, and suffocating dust during the remainder of the journey caused a great deal of illness and several deaths before they finally reached New Dwight Mission in early August.

The third and last of the spring removals involved a group of 1,070 Cherokees under the overall command of General Nathaniel Smith. Departing on June 17 in wagons, the party traveled overland to Waterloo, Alabama, where they were herded aboard boats. This collection of captive Indians was more resistant. They had heard from others of the miserable conditions aboard the riverboats, and they wanted no part of them. General Scott noted their "universal repugnance" to steamboats in a letter of June 15, 1838. The Indians had ample reason to dislike the suffocatingly crowded, dangerously leaky, and disease-infested riverboats.

The Smith migration saw large numbers of desertions. On July 3, the general wrote:

> . . . . about 300 of them threw a part of their baggage out
> of the waggons, took it and broke for the woods and
> many of the balance refused to put there baggage onto
> the waggons, or go any further and shewed much ill na-
> ture. Many of them told the agents who were with them
> that the white men were all Lyars and bad men . . . very
> many of this party were about naked, barefoot and suf-
> fering with fatigue although they had not traveled over
> 9 miles pr. day. . . .

Like the previous party, those who continued with the migration endured great suffering from heat and hunger, as well as deaths from measles and fever. There was some thought of calling them back, but it was decided that they had gone too far. The group arrived in the Indian Territory around the first of August.

Some of the Cherokees who had escaped from this company said that the Indians had had nothing whatever to eat for two days and very little before then. Six people had died before they left. The escapees told, too, of a woman so sick she could not sit up. As she lay on the ground, a soldier kicked her in the side and drove her onto the boat. Upon disembarking she was found missing and was assumed to have died en route.

The condition of these June emigrants was so bad that Cherokee leaders—headed by second chief George Lowrey, since Ross was still in Washington—sent a message to General Scott pleading that the removal be postponed until fall.

> Spare their lives, expose them not to the killing effects of that strange climate, under the disadvantages of the present inauspicious season, without a house or shelter to cover them from above, or any kind of furniture to raise them from the bare ground, on which they may spread their blankets and lay their languid limbs, when falled prostrate under the influence of disease.

In penning his memoirs in 1864, General Scott described the Cherokee holding camp at the Calhoun agency virtually as a spa, it being "twelve miles by four, well shaded, watered with perennial springs, and flanked by the Hiwassee." He did agree that many of the "poor creatures" had arrived half-starved. However, he said the cause of this was the Cherokees' own obstinate refusal to accept removal. He also claimed that the Georgians had exercised humane tenderness in rounding up the Indians and that many of them had done so with flowing tears. United Brethren missionaries J. Renatus Schmidt, Miles Vogler, and Gottlieb Rude, however, told it much differently:

> So harshly was the order executed, that no time was allowed them [the Cherokees] to take away their property, and they had the mortification to see their white neighbors, wrangling with each other for the possession of their cattle.

Beginning in early June, the entire midsection of North America was caught up in a four-months drought, with extremely high temperatures and virtually no rain. By June 19 both the Hiwassee and Tennessee rivers were so low as to be barely navigable, and the situation was worsening daily. Word arrived that the Arkansas River was in the same condition, and that the land routes had become dangerous, with drinking water extremely scarce.

Scott agreed to the Cherokees' entreaties for a delay. He ordered that the removals be halted until September 1. It was a compassionate move. But still this would mean that the remaining Indians, some 13,000 of them, would continue to be held in the poorly equipped, severely crowded, death-stricken camps through the torrid summer.

NOTES

p. 81   "I have made . . ." John Ehle, *Trail of Tears, The Rise and Fall of the Cherokee Nation* (New York: Doubleday, 1988), p. 333.

p. 82   "The Cherokees . . ." *Baptist Missionary Magazine,* 18 (September 1838): 236.

p. 83   "Georgia troops . . ." *Army-Navy Chronicle,* July 5, 19, August 2, 1838.

p. 83   "No laurel . . ." *Daily National Intelligencer,* December 14, 1838.

p. 86   ". . . about 300 . . ." Grant Foreman, *Indian Removal,* pp. 297–98.

p. 87   "Spare their lives . . " Foreman, *Indian Removal,* pp. 297–98.

p. 87   "twelve miles . . ." General Winfield Scott, "If not Rejoicing, At Least in Comfort: General Scott's Version of Removal," *Journal of Cherokee Studies* (Summer 1978): 139.

p. 87   "So harshly was . . ." *United Brethren's Missionary Intelligencer,* 7 (1842): 405.

Prisoners Without a Crime

The final massive roundup of the Cherokees was completed during June of 1838. Captain L. B. Webster was sent from Florida with orders to move 800 North Carolina Cherokees to the collection camps at Calhoun agency. He wrote to his wife from there on June 28, 1838, confessing to a sense of guilt over being one of the instruments of U.S. oppression.

> I arrived with about one hundred more than what I started with, many having joined me on the march. We were eight days in making the journey (80 miles), and it was pitiful to behold the women & children, who suffered exceedingly—as they were all obliged to walk, with the exception of the sick.

On reaching the collection points, the Cherokees were herded into the stockade pens. Many of the poorly fed and ill-cared-for captives were stricken with debilitating illnesses. Already sick with grief from losing their homes, they huddled in fear and confusion. Butrick told of being asked by an army officer to care for one group of new arrivals being collected at Brainerd:

> Accordingly, a little before sunset a company of about two hundred Cherokees were driven into our camp. The

day had been rainy, and of course all, men, women
and children, were dripping wet, with no change of
clothing, and scarcely a blanket fit to cover them.
Some of the women, when taken from their houses,
had on their poorest dress. This, of course, was the
amount of their clothing for a journey of about eight
hundred miles. As soon as permission was obtained
from the officer, we opened every door to these poor
sufferers. Mothers brought their dear little babes to
our fire, and stripped off their only covering to dry. O
how heart rending was the sight of these little sufferers. Their little lips, blue and trembling with cold,
seemed yet to force a smile of gratitude for this kind
reception. We wept and wept again, and still weep at
the thought of that offending scene.

Butrick's portrayal of the Cherokee incarceration is echoed by
the United Brethren missionaries Schmidt, Vogler, and Rude. On
a visit to the former Moravian mission site at Spring Place, they
found 200 Cherokees under a guard of soldiers. At Brainerd they
witnessed a like number who had only recently been driven across
the deep Chickamauga River, virtually like a herd of cattle. "It was
lamentable," they wrote, "to see the poor Indians with their
women and children, their sick and aged, arriving in this
drenched condition."

Military reports for July 1838 list more than 9,000 Cherokees in
the camps around the Cherokee agency at Calhoun, Tennessee.
There were 700 at the agency post, 600 at Rattlesnake Spring, 870
and 1,600 in two encampments on Mouse Creek, 900 at Bedwell
Springs, 1,300 on the Chestooee, 700 on the ridge east of the
agency, 600 on the Upper Chatate, and some 2,000 at Gunstocker
Spring.

For weeks the bewildered mass of Indians remained crammed
into the mosquito-ridden stockades without bedding, cooking
utensils, extra clothing, or adequate sanitation facilities. They
were, as Evan Jones put it, "prisoners, without a crime to justify
the fact." The few boards and bark that served as the one shelter
were wholly inadequate.

CRUEL PASSAGE

From the journal of missionary Daniel Butrick:

The weather being extremely warm and dry, many of the Cherokees are sick, especially at Calhoun, where we understand from four to ten die in a day. On returning from the camps [I] was overtaken by a gentleman with a load of dear Cherokee prisoners. Of the second boat load, he says, twenty had died when he met them at Waterloo, and great sickness was prevailing.

The Cherokees have been kept on a small spot, surrounded by a strong guard, under such circumstances that it would seem improbable for a male or female to secrete themselves from the gaze of the multitude for any purpose whatever, unless by hanging up some cloth in their tents, and there is no vessel for private use.

But now the limits are somewhat enlarged, yet it is evident that from their first arrest they were obliged to live very much like brute animals. Also, often, during their travels were obliged at night to lie down on the naked ground in the open air, exposed to wind and rain, and held together, men, women and children, like droves of hogs, and in this way are hastening to a premature grave.

Driving them under such circumstance, and then forcing them into filthy boats, to overflowing, in this hot season, leaving them at Little Rock, a most sickly place, to wait other means of conveyance 200 miles up the Arkansas river, is only a most expensive and painful way of putting the poor people to death.

The first company sent down the river, including the poor trembling doves who spent a night at our house, were, it appears, literally crammed into the boat. There was we understand, a flat bottom boat, 100 feet long, 20 feet wide, and two stories high, fastened to an old steam boat. This was so full that its timbers began to crack, and give way, and the boat itself was on the point of sinking. Some of the poor inmates were of course taken out, while the boat was lashed to the steam boat, and some other small boats were brought to take in those who had been recalled. Twelve hundred, it is said, were hurried off in this manner at one time. Who could think of crowding men, women, and children, sick and well, into a boat together, with little more room or accommodations than would be allowed swine taken to market.

Most of the Cherokees had only the clothes on their backs during three months of captivity, and these garments did little to protect against the burning heat of summer or the incessant rains and falling temperatures of autumn. Diseases, especially dysentery, stalked the crowded forts. Some Indians drank themselves into stupors with smuggled whiskey.

Extremely bad sanitary conditions, lack of washing or bathing facilities, foul drinking water, and the inadequate, unhealthy food soon led to widespread sickness. The Indians' subsistence consisted of beef, cornmeal, and some small offerings of coffee and sugar. But even that was not always available. Contractors for Indian supplies were notoriously corrupt, often providing the poorest of goods and foodstuffs.

One man, who served as an interpreter, claimed that he was in a camp one day and saw a soldier knock in the head of a barrel of crackers. The crackers, which were strewn about the ground, were moldy. The only ones who would eat them were some of the hungry children.

It has been estimated that as many as 2,500 Cherokees died while being brought in or while being held in the cramped, diseased stockades. The missionaries spent much of their time helping to bury Cherokees who had died in the camps. It was

Trail of Tears, mural by Robert Lindneux.   *(Woolaroc Museum)*

reported to Butrick that four to ten a day were dying at the Calhoun post, where a great many had become sick in their hot, crowded conditions.

Even the tribespeople who were not sick fell deeper and deeper into despair resulting from homesickness and captivity. They called the largest camp near the Cherokee agency "Aquohee" (the same name as one of their districts in North Carolina). A spokesman for the Cherokees said it meant "Captured." Always present around the confinement camps were unscrupulous whites who married Indian women to profit from government compensation. There were those who, as a Tennessee newspaper put it, strove to destroy every vestige of virtue and morality of the captive Cherokees.

At night the volunteer troops went about the stockade camps looking for Cherokee women and girls. On one occasion a group of soldiers went into a camp composed mostly of women. When the women cried out for help, the soldiers left, cursing and calling them names. The Indians were further preyed on constantly by those who used the opportunity to bilk them out of their possessions.

"Already have the Shylocks," an observer wrote, "who hovered over this terrritory while there remained food for them to prey upon, fixed their gluttonous eyes upon the frontiers, and will speedily follow the 'last Indian' to his new home."

In a letter to John Ross, George Hicks, leader of one removal caravan, indicated that once on the trail the Cherokees were still being robbed: ". . . since we have been on our march many of us have been stopped and our horses taken from our teams for the payment of unjust and past demands."

Over the years, a number of educated Cherokees had become Christian ministers. Some of these men, along with the white missionaries who remained with the Indians, stepped forward to bring a spiritual life to the camps. At Fort Butler two Cherokee Baptist ministers, Kaneeda (John Wickliffe) and O-ga-na-ya, were given permission to build a makeshift church next to the stockade. The two men and others went to work cutting and carrying posts for their building, digging holes to plant them in, and preparing temporary seating for services.

The two preached morning and night to the imprisoned Indians. Baptisms were conducted, under guard, in a nearby river. But this evidently wore thin with someone in authority. O-ga-na-ya wrote to Jones, saying: "We are in great trouble. It is said, that on Monday next we are to be arrested, and I suppose it to be true. Many are greatly terrified."

Ordained ministers Jesse Bushyhead and Stephen Foreman joined the missionaries in holding religious services at Camp Hetzel and fighting to keep the whiskey peddlers out of the compounds. When accounts began to surface that the Indians were being poorly attended in the collection camps, General Scott issued an order answering the charges:

> It is, I learn, reported that throughout this country the
> Indians collected in camps for emigration are sickly,
> and dying in great numbers. I mention this to contradict
> it. The Indians are very generally in good health, and
> so are the troops. Please cause this to be officially an-
> nounced.

The main body of Cherokees was still in the stockades when Ross returned home from Washington in July. The tribespeople were overjoyed to see him, and thousands pressed to welcome him. He was shocked to find how his Cherokee Nation had been ravaged by Scott's troops and white citizens. Ghostly homes and towns sat uninhabited except for scavengers who scurried about looting the houses, the fields, and even the graves.

Upon seeing the pathetic situation of his people, Ross went to meet Scott again at the Calhoun agency. Arguing that the Cherokees could best manage their own removal, the Cherokee leader persuaded Scott to provide an allowance of $75 per person. He further arranged the appointment of himself as superintendent of removal and subsistence. His brother Lewis would act as quartermaster. Scott agreed. He was pleased to be able to discharge the militias and reassign three of his regular regiments to other areas of need, two to Canada and one to Florida.

When Andrew Jackson—now out of office and retired to his Hermitage home near Nashville—learned of this arrangement, he howled in fury. Though feeble of hand, the old warrior penned a scathing letter to Attorney General Felix Grundy demanding that the contract with Ross be terminated and asking: "What madness and folly to have anything to do with Ross. Why is it the scamp Ross is not banished from the notice of the administration?"

In August, Ross met with other Cherokee leaders to work out plans for the removal. It was determined that the emigration would begin during September in detachments led by Cherokee men known as "conductors" and monitored by Cherokee Light Horse police. Scott agreed to provide wagons, horses, and oxen, suggesting one wagon and five saddle horses for every twenty people would be satisfactory. There should be among the Cherokees, he suggested, at least 500 strong men, women, boys, and girls capable of marching twelve to fifteen miles a day. The exercise, he said, would be good for them.

Ross responded by pointing out that after the wagons were loaded with bedding, cooking utensils, and other indispensable items needed for twenty people, the weight would prohibit more than a few persons being hauled. The two finally settled on one team and wagon and six riding horses for each fifteen people.

Ross submitted a request and won approval for compensation of $65.88 for transporting each person the entire distance. That amount was to cover wagons, horse and ox teams, food, clothing, soap, medicine, ferry and turnpike fees, and other necessities that arose on the trail. Additionally, money was allocated to cover the costs of hiring conductors, assistant conductors, physicians, commissaries, assistant commissaries, wagon masters, assistant wagon masters, and interpreters for all of the detachments.

Lewis Ross made arrangements with contractors for food and other necessities to be supplied at depots along the way. At the same time, agents for the Cherokees scoured the countryside buying wagons and teams of horses and oxen. When the animals arrived at the agency, they were branded with the initials "C N" for Cherokee Nation.

Scott's roundup of the Indians had been successful in most parts of the Cherokee country. But the troops had run into much difficulty in the Smoky Mountains of far western North Carolina. The Cherokees residing there were largely poor hill people who lived somewhat apart from the others. They seldom received as much annuity help as did the rest of their nation. The rugged, heavily wooded terrain offered many caves and other places of hiding for those wishing to escape the soldiers sent to find them.

After Scott had agreed to postpone the removal until fall, John Ross asked Jones and Bushyhead to carry a message to the leaders of the North Carolina Cherokees at Qualla. In his message, Ross urged the mountain Indians to come in and surrender themselves to the troops. Chief Yonaguska, or Drowning Bear, agreed to do so with the understanding that compliance did not mean approval of the Treaty of New Echota. During the difficult trek through the mountains, Jones and Bushyhead met a detachment of troops with 1,300 Cherokee prisoners.

"As I took some of them by the hand," Jones wrote later, "the tears gushed from their eyes."

At Fort Butler, they found some 300 more Cherokees who had just arrived from the mountains. But that was by no means the end of the story for the North Carolina natives. During the summer, some 350 of the Indians escaped from the emigration depots and fled back to the mountains. Troops were sent to the region with Indian runners whose purpose was to contact the escapees and persuade them to return. None of the Cherokees returned willingly, but about sixty were recaptured. One group that was taken prisoner, however, rebelled, killing two soldiers in the process.

Troops were sent to scout the mountains, and eventually most of the band was caught. Among them were the wife and two sons of an older Cherokee named Tsali. Tsali himself evaded capture for a time. Three of the male prisoners were blindfolded and shot by an appointed Cherokee execution squad. Later, Tsali himself was taken prisoner and executed by Cherokees who were working with the troops on the condition they would not be included in the removal. Spectators said that the old man faced his death

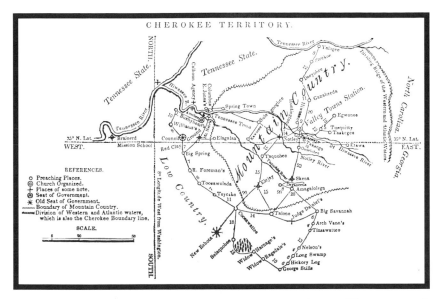

Map by Evan Jones showing sites in the Cherokee removal area of Tennessee and Georgia. (Baptist Missionary Magazine, *August, 1837*)

with a calm spirit and courage, asking only that his surviving family be cared for. It was this incident that gave rise to the famous legend of Tsali as a Cherokee folk hero, celebrated today by the outdoor pageant *Unto These Hills* at Cherokee, North Carolina.

Despite the recapture of some Cherokees, officials estimated on October 12 that some 1,400 tribespeople remained in the mountains. A large body of their descendants still reside there today.

In October the rains finally came. With winter dangerously close, it was agreed that the time had come to move. The last large body of Cherokees would bid farewell to the ancient lands of their ancestors and leave their childhood homes forever. Their homeland had been taken away by a fraudulent treaty. They had been driven from their homes and robbed of their gold fields, property, and personal possessions. They had been held in pens virtually like criminals, and they had been preyed on ruthlessly by whiskey dealers and other opportunists. Ahead now for the Cherokees was another great ordeal; the exodus that would become known to history as the Trail of Tears.

NOTES

p. 89 "I arrived . . ." Captain L. B. Webster, "Letters from a Lonely Soldier," *Journal of Cherokee Studies* (Summer 1978); 153–57.

p. 89 "Accordingly . . ." Butrick Journal, Paul Kutsche, ABC Docs., 4511: 18.3.3, vol. 4, May–June 1838.

p. 90 "It was lamentable . . ." *United Brethren's Missionary Intelligencer*, 7 (1842): 407–08.

p. 90 "prisoners . . ." *Niles Register*, August 18, 1838, p. 385.

p. 91 "The weather being . . ." Butrick Journal, Paul Kutsche, ABC Docs., 4511: 18.3.3, vol. 4, May-June 1838.

p. 93 "Already have . . ." *Daily National Intelligencer*, November 14, 1838.

p. 93 ". . . since we have . . ." Hicks to Ross, November 4, 1838, Foreman collection, OHS.

p. 94 "We are in . . ." *Baptist Missionary Magazine*, 18 (September 1838): 239.

p. 94 "It is, I learn . . ." *Army-Navy Chronicle*, August 9, 1838.

p. 95 "What madness . . ." John P. Brown, *Old Frontiers*, p. 511.

p. 96 "As I took . . ." *Baptist Missionary Magazine*, 18 (September 1838): 239.

A Trail of Tears

And so it began. On October 1, 1838, the first cavalcade of the final group moved bravely westward along the banks of the Hiwassee River. Their horse- and ox-drawn wagons were flanked on either side by horsemen and by many people on foot. The deep emotion of leaving the Cherokee homeland was expressed in the November 4, 1838 letter written by conductor George Hicks to Chief Ross:

> We are now about to take our final leave and kind fare-well to our native land, the country that the Great Spirit gave our Fathers. We are on the eve of leaving that country that gave us birth. It is the land of our Nation, and it is with sorrow that we are forced by the authority of the white man to quit the scenes of our childhood . . .

Despite the continued drought and the bad traveling conditions, the Cherokees had tried to get underway by the September 1 deadline. Two detachments set out on August 29. But when they had gone only some twenty or twenty-five miles, they were compelled by the blistering heat and scarcity of water to stop at Blythe's Ferry on the Tennessee River. General Scott called them back and reset the start at October 1.

Ross and the other chiefs had decided that the migration would follow essentially the same route as taken by the group under Lieutenant Cannon the previous fall. Undoubtedly this decision was made on the basis of terrain, roads, supply points, and river crossings. Crossing the great Mississippi River was of special concern.

In an October 8 communication, Scott outlined a general course the migration would follow. It would run down the Hiwassee River from the Calhoun agency to the Tennessee River at Blythe's Ferry, northwestward across Tennessee to Nashville. There it would turn northward to Hopkinsville and continue to Golconda, Illinois. There the route turned westward again, crossing the Mississippi River near Cape Girardeau, Missouri, and following along the Ozark ridge road of Missouri. Contrary to general thought, none of the detachments on the northern land route were escorted by U.S. troops.

Just why Scott or the Cherokees chose this much longer and far more perilous route is unclear. The Treaty party, not bound by Ross's agreement with Scott, would move directly west from Memphis across eastern Arkansas on the established road to Little Rock. The advantages of this route had been reported in a letter to the *National Intelligencer* of December 24, 1824. The letter stated that a good route had been found "making the distance of 140 miles between the two points, forty of which are through a prairie." Less than ten bridges would be required, the letter claimed, and the road could be traveled during all seasons.

Most of the groups followed the prescribed northern route, possibly because there were towns and sites along that route where supplies could be better obtained. The precise course would be up to the conductors. The previous trail experience of the Cannon group, which had been caught by winter and had suffered badly, did not offer a happy example. But neither did some of the removals by water. Ross and the other chiefs decided that the mass of people with their goods and stock would be moved best by wagon. They estimated that the 800-mile trip could be made in eighty days by traveling about ten miles a day.

The journey would thus take nearly three months. It would require being on the open road almost to the end of the year and well into winter. It was an optimistic scenario at best, failing to account for mishaps along the trail or delays caused by weather, difficult roads, rest stops, illnesses, or deaths and burials. Further, the religious dictates of the converted Cherokees who served as conductors for some groups would reject any travel on Sundays.

The chiefs divided the pro-Ross Cherokees at Calhoun into ten groups of equal size. A pro-treaty group composed an eleventh group at the agency. Some 1,029 Indians were still at Ross's Landing. Another 1,200 or more gathered at Fort Payne, Alabama would compose a twelfth overland contingent. A small final group of 231 from Alabama, removed by steamboat, would make the thirteenth.

The Alabama removal party was conducted by John Benge and aided by George Lowrey, second chief of the Nation. On September 29, Benge and Lowrey wrote to Ross from Wills Valley. They said that on the next day they would move out the first of 1,090, with three families yet to come. The commanding officer at Fort Payne had instructed them to leave by the first of October, as the fort's issuing officer would cease to distribute rations as of that date.

The letter also indicated that they had only eighty-three tents for the entire group and that two-thirds of the detachment were in a destitute condition, many being in want of shoes, clothing, and blankets as well as tents. It was hoped that additional supplies could be picked up at Huntsville, Alabama.

This detachment followed a circuitous southerly route over the Raccoon Mountains to Gunter's Landing, there fording the Tennessee River and moving north through Huntsville and on to Pulaski, Tennessee. Benge now set a direct northwesterly course for Reynoldsburg, Tennessee (then located directly east of Camden), reaching there on October 8. There had been a good deal of sickness among the emigrants. The entourage ferried over the Tennessee River at Reynoldsburg and moved on to the Iron Banks near Columbus, Kentucky, where it could cross the Mississippi, again by ferry.

Removal of Five Civilized Tribes, mural by Elizabeth James. *(Archives & Manuscripts, Oklahoma Historical Society)*

The first contingent of 36 wagons with 729 Cherokees from the Calhoun area pushed off on October 1, 1838, conducted by Daniel Colston; the second followed on October 4 with 43 wagons and 858 people under Elijah Hicks. On October 11, a week after the departure of Hicks, the pro-treaty group of between 650 and 750 Cherokees departed from the Cherokee agency area under the command of Cherokee John A. Bell. This was not a forced removal group. Not falling under the arrangement made by Ross, they were provided military escort under Lieutenant Edward Deas.

Before their departure, the other commanders complained strongly that the Bell party had been attempting to recruit emigrants from their ranks. The Ross men insisted that the pro-treaty people were falsely promising to provide land for the people in the West. Further, they said, under Ross the emigrants could get all of their $65 removal payment at the outset instead of half on departure and half on arrival. The pro-treaty people charged that Ross would personally profit in leading their removal and that he would have no land for them when they arrived.

The Bell contingent followed its own chosen course, taking the shortest and safest route to the Indian Territory. From Fort Cass the Bell detachment moved via Cleveland to Ross's Landing and took a direct westerly route through the Tennessee settlements of Winchester, Pulaski, Savannah, and Bolivar to Memphis. From there they moved across Arkansas to Little Rock and up the

Arkansas River through Conway, Russellville, and Fort Smith. Then the group continued on up the river to Fort Gibson.

Having shipped much of their baggage by boat, they moved at a leisurely pace. It took twenty-one days to travel from Memphis to Little Rock, a distance of 137 miles—making less than seven miles a day. They reached Fort Gibson on January 7, 1839, after some sixty-five days on the road.

Eight detachments followed in line from the Calhoun area during the remainder of the month and into November. In order, they were Jesse Bushyhead with 48 wagons and 135 people; Situwakee, 62 wagons and 1,250 people; Captain Old Field and later Stephen Foreman, 49 wagons and 983 people; Moses Daniel, 52 wagons and 1,035 people; James D. Wofford (Chooalooka), 58 wagons and 1,150 people; James Brown, 42 wagons and 850 people; George Hicks, 56 wagons and 1,118 people; and Peter Hildebrand, 88 wagons and 1,766 people. These counts included a good number of slaves who would suffer the journey alongside their owners. The last overland departure took place on November 7. {

Much like the captain of an ill-fated ship, John Ross remained in Tennessee until the last departure, he and his family leaving with the Hildebrand group in two carriages. He reported to General Scott on November 12 that the eleven retinues of Cherokee wagons were stretched along the trail from the Tennessee River to beyond Nashville.

One conductor complained that the proprietors of the ferry were purposely delaying the Cherokee detachment in crossing. The ferry operators, he said, were prompted by local whites who wanted the Indians held up in order to reap their treaty monies.

From Blythe's Ferry, the route climbed westward over Walden Ridge, which barricaded the Tennessee River valley on the west. Then it ran down through the Sequatchie River valley paralleling Walden Ridge, and up again across the Cumberland Plateau. It was often necessary to double-team wagons to make the steep grades.

There were other difficulties. The detachment conductors faced growing discontent and problems of morale. Always there were the unexpected breakdowns or problems that forced a decision on whether to hold up the caravan or keep to schedule. Desertions of Cherokees who chose to risk returning home were not uncommon. Many people were ill from their detention in the camps and had to be carried in the wagons. Often, contractors had not delivered forage for the animals at the required points. Bushyhead's group was detained when some of its oxen became poisoned by eating ivy; another had some of its oxen die from eating noxious weeds.

The roads at times were nothing more than layers of dust waiting to be stirred into brown, suffocating clouds. When the rains came, the rough thoroughfares turned into pits of oozing mud that clung to foot and wheel alike. Dried again, their ruts became small ravines that made travel even more difficult.

Further, there was the annoyance of having to pay excessive toll fees. The detachments paid $40 at the toll gate at Walden Ridge, and past McMinnville at the gate to the Cumberland Mountains they were hit for another 75 cents a wagon and 12½ cents for each horse—hefty prices for that day. Four of the detachments—those led by Situwakee, Old Field, Daniel, and Bushyhead—swung to the north around Murfreesboro in order to avoid the tollgates on the approach to Nashville.

On October 21, Bushyhead sent word back to Ross that he had a large number of sick people, some of them very old, who needed to be carried in wagons. Three days later, Elijah Hicks reported from near the Kentucky line that his wagon master had died at Woodbury, Tennessee. He was already short on officers to help him handle the many problems that arose daily. The old traditionalist Chief White Path, leader of White Path's Rebellion against the influence of the white man in 1827, was very ill. Of another Cherokee who had given himself up to death, Hicks wrote: "Our police has to drive him along the road sometimes fettered."

By the time the head of the emigration, the Colston and Hicks groups, reached Kentucky, winter weather had blasted in from the north. General Scott, who himself went north to attend to military matters, later spoke of the difficulties and delays endured by the emigrant parties caused by snow, ice, and resultant bad roads. "In crossing Walden's ridge and the Cumberland mountain, I found much snow as early as the 17th of November. The weather was unusually cold on the Ohio, in Kentucky, and all the way to Lake Erie . . ."

On December 28, Ross was notified that the last seven of the detachments were still in southern Illinois between the Ohio and Mississippi rivers. It was predicted that they would be forced by ice to hold up on the Mississippi. The two leading caravans under Colston and Hicks, which were ahead of the others on the northern route, arrived at their destination in January 1839. From this,

FOR WHAT CRIME?

Sitting in a frozen camp near Mt. Pleasant, Illinois on the final day of 1838, missionary Daniel Butrick reflected on the past year "of spiritual darkness" and on the plight of the Cherokee people:

> Six have died within a short time in Maj. Brown's company, and in this detachment of Mr. Taylor's. There are [people] more or less afflicted with sickness in almost every tent; and yet all are houseless & homeless in a strange land, and in a cold region, exposed to weather almost unknown in their native country. But they are prisoners. True their own chiefs have direct hold of their hands, yet the U. States offices hold the chiefs with an iron grasp, so that they are obliged to lead the people according to their directions in executing effectually that Shermerhorn [sic] treaty.
>
> But what have they done to the U. States? Have they violated any treaty? Or any intercourse law? Or abused any of the agents or officers of the U. States? Or have they refused to accommodate the U. States' citizens when passing through their country? No such thing is pretended. For what crime then was this whole nation doomed to their perpetual death?—this almost unheard of suffering? Simply because they would not agree to a principle which would be at once death to their national existence.

it is apparent that these two forward units at least managed to cross the river ahead of its freezing over. Others were stretched out behind into Kentucky.

/ A poignant description of their terrible trail conditions was provided by a traveler from Maine. His letter appeared in the *New York Observer* of January 26, 1839. He told how in November 1838 he had witnessed a body of some 1,100 Cherokees camped in a grove of woods by the roadside in southern Kentucky.

He estimated that there were sixty wagons, 600 horses, and forty pairs of oxen. A heavy rain with driving winds had hit the area, and the Indians had only their canvas wagon covers for a shield. They were already weary from the trail, and several of the older ones were suffering badly. Some were quite ill. One old man, they were told, was in the last throes of death. It was the proud old Chief White Path. He died and was buried along the road near Hopkinsville, Kentucky, his grave marked by a monument of wood painted to resemble marble. A tall pole with a linen flag was planted at the head of his grave.

The traveler met more Cherokees in early December. Even though thirty or forty of its wagons were already in camp, one caravan of 2,000 Indians plus that many animals filled the road for over three miles. The sick, feeble, and dying were in wagons. Some members rode horses, but the majority of the Indians, even elderly women, were on foot. There were those who had no shoes to protect them from the frozen ground they trod, and many struggled forward burdened with heavy packs. At every resting place, the observer learned, the Cherokees buried fourteen or fifteen of their party.

The witness from Maine also told of a woman whose youngest child was dying as they went:

> . . . she could only carry her dying child a few miles far-
> ther, and then she must stop in a stranger-land and con-
> sign her much loved babe to the cold ground, and that
> too without pomp or ceremony, and pass on with the
> multitude.

> When I past [sic] the last detachment of those suffering
> exiles and thought that my native countrymen had thus
> expelled them from their native soil and their much
> loved homes, and that too in this inclement season of the
> year in all their suffering, I turned from the sight with
> feelings which language cannot express and wept like
> childhood then.

Situwakee's fourth group, which Evan Jones had chosen to accompany, overtook and passed Bushyhead's third group. Jones, Bushyhead, and several other Cherokees were visitors at a Baptist prayer meeting in Nashville while their company paused there on November 5. Cherokees James Starr and Charles Reese, who had fought at the Battle of Horseshoe Bend, could not resist riding out to call on their old commander, Andrew Jackson, at the Hermitage, his stately home near Nashville. The former president received them graciously as they paid their respects.

Some of the Cherokees were already ill. The misery of all was increased by a torrential rain that held most of the group inside their wagons. When Ross and the Hildebrand party passed Nashville on December 2, the temperatures had begun to fall. "It is apprehended," the *Nashville Banner* commented, "that they will suffer intensely from the cold ere they reach their new homes."

The Colston, Hicks, and Situwakee groups made it across the Mississippi River before it became clogged with ice and moved on past Jackson, Missouri. On December 1, 1838, the *Southern Advocate* there reported that 1,900 Cherokees (probably the Colston and Situwakee groups, which listed some 1,929 people at the start) had passed through town the previous week. Most of them were in very bad shape.

Evan Jones posted an informative letter on December 30, 1838 from Little Prairie, Missouri, a settlement that once existed seven miles east of Rolla near the site of present St. James, Missouri.

> It has, however, been exceedingly cold for some time
> past, which renders the condition of those who are but
> thinly clad, very uncomfortable. In order, however, to
> counteract the effects of the severity of the weather in

some degree, we have, since the cold set in so severely, sent on a company to make fires along the road at short intervals. This we have found a great alleviation to the sufferings of the people.

At the Mississippi river, we were stopped from crossing, by the ice running so that the boats could not pass, for several days. Here br. Bushyhead's [third] detachment came up with us, and we had the pleasure of having our tents in the same encampment; and before our detachment got all over, Rev. Stephen Foreman's [fifth] detachment came up. I am sorry to say, however, that both detachments have not been able to cross.

I am afraid that, with all the care that can be exercised with the various detachments, there will be an immense amount of suffering, and loss of life attending the removal. Great numbers of the old, the young, and the infirm, will inevitably be sacrificed. And the fact that the removal is effected by coercion is the more galling to the feelings of the survivors.

Bushyhead and Foreman were stalled on the east bank for nearly a month, as, undoubtedly, were the other detachments behind them. A baby girl was born to Mrs. Bushyhead as her wagon train made the crossing on January 3, 1839. The new child was named Eliza Missouri Bushyhead. It was another month later, on February 3, that Reverend Bushyhead baptized three Cherokee women in the Gasconade River near present Waynesville, Missouri.

The clues offered by this and by Jones's December 30 letter indicate that the route traveled by eleven of the Tennessee groups across Missouri was much the same as that used originally by the Cannon-led party of 1837. After crossing the Mississippi River at Jonesborough, Illinois, and Cape Girardeau, Missouri, the Cherokee wagon trains followed the Ozark ridge route that had been suggested by Scott. West of the Mississippi, the trails converged at Jackson, Missouri, then moved northwestward to Farmington (probably via Fredericktown), to Caledonia (some may have gone through Potosi), west to Little Prairie, Rolla, Waynesville, Lebanon, and Springfield.

From Springfield, two routes were used: one south to Rogers, Arkansas, west to Fort Wayne in the Indian Territory, and from there to Fort Gibson. The other cut directly southwestward from Springfield to Fort Wayne and on to their particular destination.

The Fort Payne-Willstown, Alabama group did not follow the northern route. Instead, after leaving their Iron Banks crossing of the Mississippi, the detachment swung northwestward across the southeast corner of Missouri, then down into Arkansas through Smithville and Batesville and on westward to the Indian Territory via Harrison and Fayetteville.

Their party of some 1,200 with an estimated 100 wagons passed through Smithville on December 12. They had numerous cases of measles and whooping cough among them, with an average of four deaths a day. As the *Batesville News* reported on December 28, 1838, this group arrived in Batesville, Arkansas on December 15 and paused to repair their carriages, have their horses shod, and rest. The members were in destitute condition, many without shoes and other clothing. They, too, had been ravaged by the cold weather, and they had lost some fifty of their party.

John Ross had been with the Hildebrand party until it reached Paducah, Kentucky. But, because of the illness of his wife Quatie, Ross secured passage for himself and his family on the *Victoria*, which was carrying the last of the Cherokees from Alabama under the leadership of John Drew. This group had been held up on the Tennessee River from November 7 to December 4, 1838 by low water. The Rosses accompanied the group on down the Ohio and Mississippi rivers and up the Arkansas to Little Rock, where they disembarked.

It was snowy and very cold, and the Arkansas River was crusted with ice when they arrived. It is said that the ailing Quatie gave her blanket to a sick child, after which she developed pneumonia and died on February 1, 1839. Ross buried Quatie in the cemetery at Little Rock and, with his two children, pushed on overland to his destination.

The Cherokee chief had already selected a home site near Reverend Worcester's Park Hill mission, and many of his follow-

Prominent as a Cherokee merchant and Confederate officer, John Drew conducted the final group of Cherokees to the Indian Territory.   *(Archives & Manuscripts, Oklahoma Historical Society)*

ers located in the surrounding area. Many of the Cherokees from Alabama settled just north of the Arkansas River in the very southern tip of the Western Cherokee Nation. Both John Benge and George Lowrey founded new home sites in the south near the already established residence of their family relation George Guess. After the Treaty party group reached the Indian Territory, most of its members settled in the vicinity of Honey Creek in the far northeastern corner of the Cherokee lands where the Ridges and Stand Watie had established themselves earlier. ↵

NOTES

p. 99   "We are now . . ." Hicks to Ross, November 4, 1838, Foreman Collection, OHS.

p. 104   "Our police . . ." Woodward, *The Cherokees*, p. 216.

p. 105   "In crossing . . ." *House Report No. 1098*, 27th Cong., 2d sess., p. 30.

p. 105   "Six have died . . ." Butrick Journal, Paul Kutsche, ABC Docs, 4519: 18.3.3, vol. 4, December 1838.

p. 106   " . . . she could carry . . ." *New York Observer*, January 26, 1839.

p. 107   "It is apprehended . . ." *Arkansas Gazette*, December 20, 1838.

p. 107   "It has, however . . ." *Baptist Missionary Magazine*, April 1839, p. 89.

The Butrick Journal

The best descriptive accounts of Cherokee removal over the northern route are provided by the letters and diaries of the missionaries. Evan Jones and Daniel Butrick rode with the Cherokees during the infamous march and made records of the suffering and death. Though the United Brethren missionaries traveled by themselves just ahead of the large caravans—and in front of the winter blasts—their narratives of the trail and the condition of the Western Cherokees on their arrival are important contributions to the lore of the removal.

It was Butrick who provided the most detailed and compelling account. A native of Windsor, Massachusetts, he and his wife had come to Brainerd mission school as Presbyterian missionaries for the American Board of Commissioners for Foreign Missions in January 1817. Strongly believing that the only way to really help the Cherokees was to learn their language, history, and culture, he had given up the comforts of Brainerd to live with an old-style Cherokee family. He was far more willing than his fellow missionaries to climb aboard a horse and visit the remotest families of the Cherokee Nation to preach the gospel. Once he had learned the language, which he found to be full of richness and beauty, he proceeded to translate the New Testament. A close friend of

Baptist Evan Jones, Butrick was sympathetic to the poorest of the Cherokees and appalled at the growing class separation between rich and poor.

Because of his opposition to the New Echota treaty, Butrick had not been approved by the American Board to go west with the Cherokees. But there was no question that he would follow. The minister's love and friendship for the Cherokees ran true and deep; the Indians were his doves, his life's work. His compassion and concern are clearly evident in his personal journal as he labored to care for them in the holding camps at Ross's Landing and as he traveled with them over the Trail of Tears.

Butrick remained behind as long as possible, tending the ill, burying the dead, preaching the gospel, and defying as best he could the evil work of his fellow whites.

"The white men in this country," he wrote, "generally seem devoid of moral principle, and I do sometimes doubt whether any true Christian has ever been left to unite in the present method of robbing the Indians of this country."

He and other ministers strongly opposed to the Treaty of New Echota met with their congregations to adopt resolutions not to join in Christian fellowship with any of the people who had signed the treaty unless they first confessed to their sin. Nor would they recognize Reverend Schermerhorn, negotiator of the treaty, as a minister or even as a common Christian. "No one favoring the treaty," Butrick wrote bitterly, "has a true love of God, including Boudinot."

Butrick and his wife were members of the next-to-last group to leave. This was the detachment commanded by Cherokee conductor Richard Taylor. It set forth from Ross's Landing on November 1. The Butricks, he on horseback and his wife in a one-horse carryall, rode with the caravan as it made its way north along the west bank of the Tennessee River until turning westward onto the Nashville Road.

Trouble went with the group. A wagon that broke and spilled its load of corn onto the ground had to be repaired and its cargo retrieved. Word that the Cherokees had received some of their treaty money spread quickly, and white whiskey dealers trailed the wagon train with barrels of whiskey to sell to the Indians. A band of young Cherokees under Big Dollar drank, yelled, and sang all through the night. They ruined the minister's sleep and upset him greatly with their blasphemous language. One Cherokee became so drunk that he lay down too close to a fire and burned himself badly. He died later on down the trail.

After crossing the Sequatchie River valley, the party camped at the foot of Cumberland Mountain. Again they were beseiged by whiskey dealers. The caravan paused here so that the long line of wagons could be prepared for the mile-and-a-half climb up the steep grade. The train was fortunate that in making the climb only one wagon turned over. They went into camp near a farmhouse atop the plateau. There a rainstorm blew water into their wagons, soaking their clothes. When the travelers rose the next morning, some from tents but most from blankets on the ground, they found that a light snow had fallen.

The descent of the mountain, at times with rock cliffs on one side and deep abysses on the other, was even more precarious than the ascent. Butrick was greatly concerned that the teamsters would lose control of the heavy wagons. But the convoy continued on slowly without mishap to the Collins River. There women did laundry while men gathered firewood and took care of what blacksmithing the wagons required.

Beyond the Collins, they camped near McMinnville, which Butrick found to be a pleasant village surrounded by log-house farms with large herds of cattle. From there, however, rain started, and continued most of the day and into another stormy night. Soon after they had pitched their tents, a large band of white people arrived, "as eager, apparently, for money, as ever birds of prey were for a dead carcass." Some of the white men crowded around the detachment's campfire, virtually taking possession of it.

Butrick and his wife sometimes found temporary respite from the hardships of the trail in homes along the way. But the minister lamented the plight of the Indians, who had begun to suffer badly from the continued exposure and wear of their travels. "The poor sick Cherokees," he observed, "cannot stop and be refreshed by kind friends as we were at Woodbury, but must be exposed to die." Indeed, the second casualty of the journey occurred when

John Ross's gravesite, Park Hill, Oklahoma. *(Photo by Stan Hoig)*

John Goodmoney took ill and expired shortly before the Cherokee wagon caravan passed through Murfreesboro.

At Nashville, Butrick, along with Evan Jones of Bushyhead's group and other churchmen, laid plans to hold a religious gathering of their flocks. A Nashville Baptist minister came forth to offer them the use of a brick building for the meeting. The minister and his parishioners also contributed clothing and much-needed tents for the homeless Cherokees as they took up their march northwestward into winter-struck Kentucky.

Moving at a rate of only some sixty miles a week, Taylor's party reached Hopkinsville, Kentucky on December 1 and went into camp. The weather had grown much colder. Butrick now began recording an increasing number of deaths, mainly from among the old and infirm and children. Dysentery and whooping cough were spreading among more and more of the party. By the time the group reached the Ohio River across from Golconda, Illinois, some fifteen of its members had perished, adding to a reported sixty persons from the detachments that had preceded them.

Butrick's caravan had already passed some of the Wofford people who were still in camp at Princeton, Kentucky. That group was reportedly in disarray because of Wofford's heavy drinking. There was more disturbance caused by alcohol as the caravans approached the Ohio River settlements. On one occasion Butrick witnessed a Cherokee Light Horse unit arrest and tie up one raging whiskey drinker. Later the Indian police charged off after another band of drunken men.

Other Cherokees, distraught and bitter at their fate, refused to hold communion with Butrick, leading him to think about what lay ahead for him in the new land. He wrote:

> I have no pleasing anticipation about arriving on the Arkansas. Mr. Worcester will doubtless wish to sustain, or at least excuse, Mr. Boudinot in the course he had taken; and as the A. Board have received Mr. Boudinot as an assistant missionary at the West, they doubtless look over his conduct in making the treaty. Yet the mission churches do not.

Elias Boudinot's grave marker near Tahlequah, Oklahoma. *(Photo by Stan Hoig)*

It was mid-December when the Taylor company crossed the Ohio River. They made it just in time. The Hildebrand wagon train, now last in line, was prevented from crossing by floating ice in the river. Reports came, too, that other groups were similarly stymied by the Mississippi River. "It is distressing," Butrick observed, "to think on the situation of the Nation. One detachment stopped at the Ohio River. Two at the Mississippi; one four miles this side, one 16 miles this side, one 18 miles, and one 13 miles behind us."

Among some 8,000 souls, he noted, there was now a vast amount of sickness and many deaths. Rampant dysentery had rendered people weak and shivering in their all-too-thin blankets. Six members of the James Brown party had died within a short time, and there was illness in almost every tent.

Taylor's group remained in camp in Illinois until late January. Word came that two of the forward detachments had finally crossed the Mississippi. When Hildebrand moved forward, the Taylor company decamped and made its way to the bank of the Mississippi at Jonesboro, Illinois. Despite rain and a snowstorm, they began crossing the great river by boat on January 28, 1839. Continued ice flow, however, stymied the effort when about half the Cherokees were across. It would be three weeks before the task was completed.

During that time, five members died. A few days down the trail, Butrick recorded the deaths of one old Cherokee woman, one black man, and three Cherokee children. Almost every night he would tally the day's casualties: Drowning Bear, dead; the wife of Wiley Bigbee, dead; the wild, young Lewis Perdue, dead; an old man and a child, the daughter of Archibald Fields, dead; another night, two more children, dead. Butrick wrote of a family that had come to a trailside prayer meeting. A ten- to twelve-year-old boy was very ill with a bowel complaint. "He extended his emaciated hand to take mine, then pointed to the place of his extreme pain. Before our meeting was closed, he was a corpse."

Funerals were conducted at almost every camping spot. At times a victim would be found dead in one of the wagons and would be laid to rest in the dark of night. Firewood was often scarce, and it was difficult to find boards to make "something of a coffin."

For the next eight weeks. Butrick's caravan of rattling wagons and bent, stumbling Indians would push across the sparsely occupied countryside of southern Missouri. They were encamped west of Farmington, eighty miles beyond the Mississippi River, when Taylor was called back to a meeting with Chief Ross and other conductors at Jonesboro. Concerned over unexpected delays and expenses, Ross urged the men to travel on Sunday at times.

As the wagon train pushed on westward, the weather fluctuated wildly. It would rain for two or three days, then clear up for a brief period of sunshine, followed by a sudden change to blizzardlike cutting winds and bitter cold. Wintry blasts from the north would blow down tents, permitting rain to soak the bedding and clothes. Dropping temperatures and snow would follow behind. The Butricks, themselves often finding refuge in the homes of whites along the way, prayed for the poor suffering Cherokees, who could find no relief from their tortures on the trail.

Taylor's caravan followed a route that passed through Jackson, Farmington, and Caledonia, Missouri, and then on to the Gasconade River. This more direct route cut south of that taken by most of the other detachments. As they neared Springfield, word came that Hildebrand, who was also following a cutoff route, was intending to cut in ahead of them on the main road.

The Hildebrand caravan had departed from the established route across Missouri fifteen miles west of Caledonia. It, too, had slanted southwestern more directly for Springfield, striking the route followed by other parties near present-day Marshfield, Missouri, after Taylor had passed. In order to stay in front of the Hildebrand party, Taylor put his people on the trail early each morning and traveled on Sunday.

Beyond Springfield the wagon train turned southwestward into Arkansas and diagonally across the northwest corner of that state. They did not pass through Fayetteville as had others. The bitter cold, the sickness, and the deaths continued throughout the

A PARTICIPANT'S STORY

From an unidentified source, reported April 7, 1929 in the *Daily Oklahoman:*

Long time we travel on way to new land. People feel bad when they leave Old Nation. Womens cry and made sad wails. Children cry and many men cry, and all look sad like when friends die, but they say nothing and just put heads down and keep on go toward west. Many days pass and people die very much. My father, now old man, is walking along and all of sudden fall down in snow and can't get up. One day he live in covered wagon and then is dead. We bury him close by trail and go on. A week passes and my mother cry out one day and fall over. She speak no more and we bury her and go on. Three weeks pass by and my two brothers and three sisters all get sick and die, one each day and all are gone. We bury them by trail and go on. Lots of others die every day and so we go on. We bury and march. Soon there is more dead and we bury more and keep on. Looks like maybe all be dead before we get to new Indian country, but always we keep marching on and all time there is new cry made from wagons where is old people and children. All day and all through night is cry and moan. Seem like I still hear cries and moans after so many years gone past. People sometimes say I look like I never smile, never laugh in lifetimes. No, I used to smile and laugh in long go times, but no man has laugh left after he's marched over long trail from Old Nation to new country in west. Guess maybeso I will laugh no more while living, but when new land is reached in skies and all my people is meet me again then no think I make joyful laugh.

Long time I am live in hills and many good people live close by, but most of time I am thinking of Old Nation and wonder how big mountain now looks in springtime, and how the boys and young men used swim in big river, and go on hunts far down in great valley, and then there come before picture of march on long trail what led to far west and then my heart feel heavy and sad. Maybeso some day we will understand why Cherokees had to suffer on trail to new country.

journey until March 24. On that day the detachment finally reached its destination at a place just inside the Indian Territory known as Woodhall's. This point, near present-day Westville, Oklahoma, was twenty-four miles east of the Park Hill mission that had been established by the Reverend Samuel A. Worcester in 1837.

Government records indicate that the Elijah Hicks group, the second to depart from the Calhoun agency, had arrived in the Indian Territory on January 4, 1839, after 93 days on the trail. It was followed on January 11 by the Alabama Cherokees in 103 days. Making a loop across southeast Missouri, the Benge/Lowrey-led wagon train had swung down to Smithville and Batesville, Arkansas, and then pushed due west through Fayetteville to the Indian Territory.

Colston's lead-off party arrived on January 17 after 109 days on the trail, followed by Situwakcc on February 2 after 106 days; the Old Field/Foreman group on February 23 after 127 days; and Jesse Bushyhead on February 27 after 135 days. The remainder all arrived in March: Wofford, March 1, 127 days; James Brown, March 5, 130 days; George Hicks, March 14, 131 days; John Drew's boat people, March 18, 104 days; Taylor, March 24, 139 days; and Hildebrand, March 25, 139 days.

Butrick left the Taylor company soon after arrival, making his way to Fairfield Mission, which had been established by Dr.

Cherokee Nation Capitol building at Tahlequah, Oklahoma. *(Photo by Stan Hoig)*

Marcus Palmer in 1829 south of present-day Stigler, Oklahoma. During 1839 Butrick founded a small school at Breadtown near Westville. He continued to be a staunch opponent of the Treaty party men, speaking out against the compromise position of Worcester and of the American Board itself.

Making the journey to the West was only part of the Cherokee tragedy. Upon arrival they were often weak and ill from the journey. They found themselves in an unsettled land without shelter, adequate food, or proper medical attention. More of them would soon perish. The number of Cherokees who died during their roundup, while in the various collection camps, on the Trail of Tears, or soon after as a result of the removal ordeal will never be known.

A physician who accompanied one group estimated that 2,000 of the 16,000 removed, or one-eighth of the total number, had died after they were taken from their homes and began to decamp for emigration. The figure of 4,000 has often been used in relation to the camp and trail deaths. There is no possibility of obtaining hard figures. A government report showed a total of 447 estimated deaths for the thirteen detachments in the camps and during removal, with no record for three of them. This is unquestionably a very low estimate. It does indicate, though, that at least that many died.

But at some point, the numbers become moot. The cruel banishment was a disaster for the Cherokee Nation, not alone in cost of human life, but also in the enormous loss of ancient homeland, in personal property, and in tribal autonomy. It would soon become apparent that the Cherokees had suffered what was probably their greatest calamity as a direct result of their removal.

NOTES

p. 113   "The white men . . ." Butrick Journal, Paul Kutsche, ABC Docs., 4519: 18.3.3, vol. 4, October 1838.

p. 113   "No one . . ." Butrick Journal, Paul Kutsche, ABC Docs., 4517: 18.3.3, vol. 4, October, 1838.

P. 114   "as eager . . ." Butrick Journal, Paul Kutsche, ABC Docs., 4519: 18.3.3, vol. 4, December 1838.

p. 115   "The poor sick . . ." Butrick Journal, Paul Kutsche, ABC Docs., 4519: 18.3.3, vol. 4, December 1838.

p. 116   "I have no . . ." Butrick Journal, Paul Kutsche, ABC Docs., 4519: 18.3.3, vol. 4, December 1838.

p. 118   "It is distressing . . ." Butrick Journal, Paul Kutsche, ABC Docs., 4519: 18.3.3, vol. 4, December 1838.

p. 118   "He extended . . ." Butrick Journal, Paul Kutsche, ABC Docs., 4521: 18.3.3, vol. 4, February 12 to March 23, 1839.

p. 120   "Long time we . . ." *Daily Oklahoman*, April 7, 1929.

Painful Aftermath

The United Brethren ministers Schmidt, Vogler, and Rude had arrived in the Indian Territory on October 27, 1838, well ahead of the Old Nation exodus. They found the Treaty party Cherokees who had removed earlier now settled into homes on Honey Creek and at Park Hill, where Reverend Samuel Worcester had established his new mission. They visited with Stand Watie and his brother Thomas, Elias Boudinot, and Major and John Ridge as well as General Matthew Arbuckle at Fort Gibson.

They also found that nearby to the north were some 500 Indians, remnants of the Senecas and other Six Nation tribes, whom the government had brought to the Territory from the New York and Great Lakes region. These Indians were suffering badly from disease, fever, and alcohol consumption. Present also was the first contingent of Creeks, whom the government had earlier assigned to much the same area as the Cherokees. An epidemic of the dreaded smallpox was spreading among them rapidly.

Soon after the first of the year, the Old Nation Cherokees began arriving in the Indian Territory, homeless and bewildered, with many still sick or dying. Despite its promises, the U.S. government was ill-prepared to fulfill its treaty obligations to feed and care for them. Subsistence for the more than 12,000 refugees had been assigned to independent contractors, who enlarged their profits with low-cost, inferior supplies. The flour and meal were often infested with weevils, and the meat spoiled. When George Hicks's detachment arrived at Beattie's Prairie in the Cherokee Nation on March 14, he wrote to Ross: "We are informed that they have some shelled corn and some very poor beef for our Subsistence which is unfit for use & from the promises made to us in the Nation East we did not Expect such Treatment."

Ross complained to Cherokee agent Montfort Stokes that the contractors had established distribution depots at remote points that were extremely difficult for the tribespeople to reach. He noted that the detachment that had arrived by water had been issued fifteen days' rations and assured that a depot would soon be established. However, when the fifteen days of provisions had been used up, no arrangements had been made to supply more. Receiving no help from Stokes, Ross made a plea to General Arbuckle, commanding at Fort Gibson, for a speedy remedy for the starvation his people faced.

Neither Stokes nor Arbuckle was able to provide any supplementary assistance. At exorbitant Indian Territory prices, Ross was forced to use funds allotted to him by General Scott for emigration to purchase provisions that the Cherokees desperately required: food, housing materials, furniture, plows, and other items essential in reestablishing their lives in the West.

The Cherokee story was only one part of the mass dislocation of Northern and Southern Indian tribes by the United States during the first half of the nineteenth century. Many other tribes suffered their own anguish and loss of life in being ejected from their native territories and driven off to new lands in the West. Always the tribes were given assurances much the same as those President James Monroe had given the Cherokees in 1817:

> As long as water flows, or grass grows upon the earth,
> or the sun rises to show your pathway, or you kindle
> your camp fires, so long shall you be protected by this
> Government, and never again removed from your pre-
> sent habitations.

ELIAS BOUDINOT, CHEROKEE INTELLECTUAL

When Elias Boudinot died at the hands of assassins, the Cherokee Nation lost one of its most outstanding intellectuals. The one-time editor of the *Cherokee Phoenix* had taken a stand in favor of removal in the belief that it was best for his people. For doing so, he paid with his life.

Boudinot had been born in 1804 in northern Georgia. His English name was Buck Waite; in Cherokee it was Gallegina. After early schooling at the Moravians' Spring Place Mission, he had been one of the first Cherokees selected to attend the Foreign Mission School at Cornwall, Connecticut. Escorted east by Jeremiah Evarts of the American Board of Foreign Missions, Buck was taken en route to meet Thomas Jefferson at Monticello, James Madison at Montpelier, and Elias Boudinot in New Jersey.

The elderly Boudinot, former president of the Continental Congress and then head of the American Bible Society, was impressed with the fifteen-year-old Cherokee boy. It was at his suggestion that Buck took up the name of Elias Boudinot as his own.

At Cornwall, and later at the Andover Theological School, the Cherokee boy grew into a good-looking man of learning and high values. There he also met and married Harriet Gold, the daughter of a missionary, afterward returning with his bride to the Cherokee Nation. There he began the work of a missionary and teacher.

In 1826, Boudinot made a speaking tour of southern and eastern cities to raise funds with which to buy a printing press and have Sequoyah's new syllabary cast in type. He also pleaded the cause for the humanness of his race. When the Cherokee Nation set out to establish its newspaper in 1827, the *Cherokee Phoenix,* he was hired as the first editor.

Boudinot quickly proved to be a capable and enterprising editor, not only providing the news and editorial content in English, but translating it into Cherokee. He also worked with missionary Samuel Worcester in publishing a Cherokee-language book of religious hymns and a translation of Matthew's gospel from the Bible.

It is fair to say that what Sequoyah did for the Cherokees in language and Ross did for them in politics, Boudinot did for his people with the printed word. He used it to foster religion, to inform and educate the Cherokees, to express Cherokee views to outsiders, and to fight against the injustices heaped on them.

When the State of Georgia threatened to pass a series of laws restricting the Cherokees, Boudinot wrote in the March 6, 1828 *Phoenix:* "Who will expect the Cherokees to make a rapid progress in education, religion, agriculture, and the various arts of civilized life when resolutions are passed to wrest their country from them."

Boudinot eventually concluded, however, that it was hopeless for the Cherokees to try to exist under such conditions and that it was best for them to remove to the West—even if the Cherokee masses were not wise enough to see it. "If one hundred persons are ignorant of their true situation," he wrote in the May 22, 1838 *National Intelligencer,* "and are so completely blinded as not to see the destruction that awaits them, we can see strong reasons to justify the actions of a minority of fifty persons to do what the majority *would* do if they understood their condition, to save a *nation* from political thralldom and degradation."

The Cherokee intellectual had thrust himself into the most passionate issue of Cherokee concern. The loss of homeland had created intense intratribal hatreds. Following removal to the Indian Territory, many Cherokees felt betrayed, and there were demands for vengeance. On June 22, 1839, as he was overseeing the building of a new home near present-day Tahlequah, Oklahoma, an assassin plunged a knife into Boudinot's back. Today his grave at Park Hill helps to mark the journey's end on the Trail of Tears.

The Indian Territory had been established as a sanctuary for tribes that originally lived east of the Mississippi. At first it encompassed lands in Kansas and Nebraska, but it had become restricted largely to what is now the state of Oklahoma. Once there, the Cherokees came together with tribes from both the northern and southern tier of the East who had been similarly uprooted and sent west on their own Trails of Tears.

In the north the Indian tribes had at first been pushed away from the Atlantic seaboard and relocated beyond the Appalachian Mountains. This country south of the Great Lakes was soon prized by white settlers, and the Indians were forced farther west. During the War of 1812, some of the tribes, united under the great Tecumseh, attempted to hold their ground by siding with the British. But the Indians were severely defeated by U.S. forces under General William H. Harrison, and their punishment was banishment beyond the Mississippi River.

In the South, other tribes suffered fates similar to that of the Cherokees. Whereas Jefferson and his immediate successors attempted to remove the Indians by voluntary means, Andrew Jackson was more determined. Immediately upon his election in 1828, he pushed his Indian Removal Bill through Congress and set about to initiate new treaties with the Southern tribes, employing the usual technique of bribing chiefs in order to trade lands in the West for the Indians' homelands.

By these treaties, the Creeks were removed from southern Alabama, the Choctaws from southern Mississippi, and the Chickasaws from northern Mississippi and western Tennessee. It took a war to uproot the Seminoles from Florida, but during the decade of the 1830s, they and the other tribes were moved to the Indian Territory.

Virtually all of the tribes had known misery and loss of life similar to what the Cherokees experienced. "By persuasion and force," Andrew Jackson himself admitted regarding the tribes, "they have been made to retire from river to river, and from mountain to mountain, until some of the tribes have become extinct and others have left but remnants."

By any measure, removal of the tribes had been a national disgrace. For the most part, the government had assigned the feeding and transporting of the Indians to private contractors, who were often relatives of high officials. With no oversight, the system was an open invitation to profiteering and fraud at the expense of the defenseless people.

When cries of protest began flooding Washington, President Martin Van Buren sent Major Ethan Allen Hitchcock to the Indian Territory to investigate. The appointment was a mistake; Hitchcock was much too honest a person to whitewash the injustices he found. He toured the Territory and talked with Indians and whites alike. His report, solidly supported with evidence, was a catalogue of abuses perpetrated on the Indians by officials and contractors.

Hitchcock found far more corruption than he had ever expected. Beef issued to the Indians was often spoiled and rotten; blankets supplied them were of poorest quality; and false scales and measures were used to claim twice as much issue of corn or salt as was actually made. White men regularly made great profits by duping naive tribespeople who had no concept of the value of American dollars.

When cattle were supplied, they had often been so poorly fed that they were too weak to stand up. Exaggerated weights for the animals were given, making for overcharging. Sometimes the cows were recaptured by the contractors and reissued. Interpreters were bribed to help defraud the uneducated victims. Worn-out oxen were forced on them at exorbitant prices.

Blacksmiths and wheelwrights, who were paid good salaries by the government to work for the tribes, often demanded extra pay for any work they did. Indian agents, contractors, and others employed bribery, kickbacks, forgery, and perjury to reap thousands of dollars in nefarious profits. Those who tried to deal honestly with the Indians were often dismissed.

Worse still, Creek trader James Edwards told Hitchcock, the chiefs and mixed-bloods were often rewarded to prevent complaint. Meanwhile the common, uneducated Indians were left to survive as best they could. In the treaties for removal, a certain class of the tribes had been declared incompetent to manage their share of the payments. Government officials became "voluntary agents" for handling the Indians' moneys. As a result, the less educated and poorer Indian was usually the more cheated and abused.

Particularly helpless and unattended were orphaned children and widows. The health of Creek women had been so badly damaged in the removal, Edwards claimed, that no infants had been seen among the tribe for nearly two years.

Hitchcock filled nine notebooks with information regarding the Indians and their situation in the Indian Territory. Returning to Washington, he submitted a scathing report of his findings, supported by a hundred pieces of evidence, to the secretary of war. Though Hitchcock's personal diaries remain, the official report mysteriously disappeared and has not been seen since.

Deep animosities had been created among the Cherokees by the Treaty of New Echota and the selling of the Old Nation lands. Lurking still in the recesses of Cherokee culture were the ancient traditions of blood revenge. On June 22, 1839, Major Ridge, John Ridge, and Elias Boudinot were brutally assassinated by other Cherokee tribesmen.

It would take years, for some a lifetime, for the scars of the removal and the Trail of Tears to fade away. Intratribal hatreds that kept the Cherokees in a state of virtual anarchy for a time were too deeply embedded to dissolve quickly. But in 1846 the federal government worked out a peace agreement among the Cherokee factions. A blessed calm came to the Cherokee Nation. With the rancor quieted and the trauma of the removal finally behind them, the Cherokee Nation could turn to rebuilding itself.

During this pre–Civil War period, they built themselves a fine courthouse, created an orphanage, established both a male and a female seminary, and gradually became more and more prosperous. Some likened this rebirth to that of the great phoenix bird of mythology that rose from its own ashes to begin a new life of immortality.

The golden period would last for fifteen years—until the white man would again bring disunion, death, and destruction to the Cherokees with the Civil War. Once again the Cherokees became chaotically split, some fighting with the Union and some with the Confederacy. The havoc and bitter dissention of the war may have rivaled even that of the removal. Yet for the Cherokees, and for the many other tribes that underwent a similar tragedy in being exiled from their native lands, the Trail of Tears remains as a symbol of the injustice done them.

NOTES

p. 125   "We are informed . . ." Gary E. Moulton, ed., *The Papers of John Ross* (Norman: University of Oklahoma Press, 1985), vol. I, p. 701.

p. 125   "As long as . . ." *Daily National Intelligencer*, March 3, 1854.

p. 128   "By persuasion . . ." John Barlett Meserve, "The Indian Removal Message of President Jackson," *Chronicles of Oklahoma*, 12 (March 1935): 64.

Selected Further Reading List

Nonfiction

Anderson, William L., ed. *Cherokee Removal, Before and After*. Athens: University of Georgia Press, 1991. Provides six essays on Cherokee removal and the Trail of Tears plus a bibliographical essay on Cherokee publications.

Bass, Althea. *Cherokee Messenger*. Norman: University of Oklahoma Press, 1936. A biography of missionary Samuel Worcester backgrounding the Cherokee conflict with Georgia.

Brill, Marlene Targ. *The Trail of Tears: The Cherokee Journey from Home*. Brookfield, Conn.: Millwood Press, 1995. An account of the Cherokee removal written for a juvenile audience.

Carter, Samuel, III. *Cherokee Sunset: A Nation Betrayed*. Garden City, N.Y.: Doubleday, 1976. A readable history of the Cherokees and their relations with the United States beyond their removal.

Cwiklik, Robert. *Sequoyah and the Cherokee Alphabet*. Morristown, N.J.: Silver Burdett Press, 1989. A fictionalized biography of Sequoyah.

Ehle, John. *Trail of Tears: The Rise and Fall of the Cherokee Nation*. New York: Doubleday, 1988. A general history of the Cherokees, somewhat fictionalized. Available in paperback.

Foreman, Grant. *Indian Removal: The Emigration of the Five Civilized Tribes*. Norman: University of Oklahoma Press, 1932. An account of the removal of the tribes from the South to the Indian Territory.

———. *Sequoyah*. Norman: University of Oklahoma Press, 1938. A primary study of the man who invented the Cherokee alphabet.

Gibson, Arrell, ed. *America's Exiles: Indian Colonization in Oklahoma*. Oklahoma City: Oklahoma Historical Society, 1976. A series of researched essays on removal of the various tribes and their ensuing conditions.

Hoig, Stan. *Sequoyah, the Cherokee Genius*. Oklahoma City: Oklahoma Historical Society, 1995. A newly researched account of Sequoyah's life.

Jahoda, Gloria. *The Trail of Tears: The Story of the American Indian Removals 1813–1855*. New York: Holt, Rinehart and Winston, 1975. A stylized history of tribal removals.

McLoughlin, William G. *After the Trail of Tears*. Chapel Hill: University of North Carolina Press, 1993. A study of the Cherokees after their arrival in Oklahoma.

———. *Cherokees and Missionaries, 1789–1839*. New Haven: Yale University Press, 1984. An account of missionary work among the Cherokees.

Moulton, Gary E. *John Ross, Cherokee Chief*. Athens: University of Georgia Press, 1978. A biography of the Cherokees' most important chief.

Perdue, Theda. *The Cherokee*. New York: Chelsea House, 1989. A good, well-illustrated narrative of Cherokee culture and history.

Shumate, Jane. *Sequoyah, Inventor of the Cherokee Alphabet*. New York: Chelsea House, 1994. A young-reader account of the famous Cherokee inventor.

Woodward, Grace Steele. *The Cherokees*. Norman: University of Oklahoma Press, 1963. A readable, well-documented history of the Cherokees.

Fiction

Barrett, Stephen Melvil. *Joe the Cherokee*. New York: E. P. Dutton, 1944. The story of a boy whose family dies on the Trail of Tears.

Booker, Jim. *The Trail to Oklahoma*. Nashville: Broadman, 1959. A young-reader story of a Cherokee boy on the Trail of Tears.

Conley, Robert J. *Mountain Windsong*. Norman: University of Oklahoma Press, 1992. A novel of the Trail of Tears by a native Cherokee writer.

Daves, Frances M. *Cherokee Worman*. Boston: Branden Press, 1973. The story of a Georgia Cherokee family caught up in the great removal.

Heischmann, Glen. *While Rivers Flow*. New York: The Macmillan Co., 1963. A historical novel of a U.S. Army officer who is forced into the brutal removal of the Cherokees, whom he has come to love and respect.

Hoobler, Dorothy and Thomas. *The Trail on Which They Went*. New York: Silver Burdett, 1992. The story of a Cherokee girl on the Trail of Tears.

Stewart, Elizabeth J. *The Long Trail Home*. New York: Clarion Books, 1994. Tale of a boy who escapes from his captors on the Trail of Tears.

Index

Entries are filed letter by letter. **Boldface** page references indicate boxed features. *Italic* page references indicate illustrations and captions.